"Uncle Tom's Story of His Life."
by Josiah Henson

Address:
HardPress
8345 NW 66TH ST #2561
MIAMI FL 33166-2626
USA
Email: info@hardpress.net

"UNCLE TOM'S"
STORY OF HIS LIFE
From 1789 to 1876
EDITED BY JOHN LOBB.

REV. JOSIAH HENSON
(Mrs. Harriet Beecher Stowe's "Uncle Tom").

LONDON:
"CHRISTIAN AGE" OFFICE, 89, FARRINGDON ST.

W 49.
.584
.45

LIBRARY

OF THE

College of New Jersey.

PRESENTED BY

JOHN S. PIERSON, A. M.

OPINIONS OF THE PRESS.

"We do not need to inform our readers who 'Uncle Tom' is; we lately announced his presence in this country, at the advanced age of eighty-eight. Those who have heard him will not require any persuasion to make a closer acquaintance with his remarkable career, as it is set forth in this 'Story.' It proves conclusively that Mrs. Beecher Stowe's famous 'Uncle Tom's Cabin' is in no sense overdrawn; indeed it would hardly be possible to exaggerate on the subject. Our first feeling on reading this 'Story' would have been one of amazement that human beings could become such incarnate fiends as some of the slave-holders and overseers are here represented to be, were it not that recent history has brought to light yet blacker deeds of cruelty and shame. Our second feeling was one of thankfulness to God that in America at least such experiences as those of 'Uncle Tom' can never be repeated. Mr. Henson tells the story of his life—his ups and downs, his sufferings, his escape, his subsequent career—in short the sorrows of his race—with a pathos and dramatic force that are perfectly astounding when his early training is considered. We wish this book (which is well got up and adorned with photographs of the author and Mrs. Stowe) a large circulation; we wish, too, that Mr. Henson's present mission to England may be as successful as he could desire."—*The Christian,* Nov. 23rd, 1876.

"This is the autobiography of the Rev. Josiah Henson, whose history furnished Mrs. Beecher Stowe with some of the incidents out of which grew the story and character of her 'Uncle Tom.' The 'story' is instructive and interesting, full as it is of 'moving incidents by flood and field'—showing what may be done by energy and faith even by an untutored slave labouring under the greatest disadvantages; indeed, if we did not know that it told the events of real life, we should take it as a stirring romance written for our delectation and amusement. It is well compiled and produced, and makes an elegant addition to the table."

"This autobiography is illustrated by capital portraits of its subject, the Rev. Josiah Henson, and of Mrs. Harriet Beecher Stowe, as is most befitting such a volume. Most of our readers well know that the veritable 'Uncle Tom' is at this moment in England, and in London. This day (Tuesday) the writer of this notice met him at the bottom of Fleet Street, looking hale and hearty, and self-possessed, though now in his eighty-eighth year. One could not help wishing such a fine old man might live till he was a hundred years old, if it please God to spare his life so long. At his present advanced age there is manliness in his bearing, calmness in the expression of his countenance, and firmness in his step. His whole demeanour indicates that he is no common man. Though he has lost much of the suppleness and brightness of his race, and a good deal of the elasticity and fire of his best days, he is evidently 'all there' yet. Though he is now 'Uncle Tom' the aged, he is still every bit a man. Large numbers in the metropolis will hear his voice, but vastly larger numbers will read the story of his life. It matters not where one opens the book, one cannot lay it down again. It opens the fountains of one's heart and eyes, and one cannot help thanking God that such a son of Ham ever endured the lash, or trod the swamps of America. His trials were hard for flesh and blood to bear; but God had a work for him to do, and he has faithfully borne witness to the grand truths of the Gospel. Before we give an extract from this thrilling narrative—and we scarcely know where to select, or rather where not to select—we may mention that within the first twenty-four hours of its publication, two thousand copies of the book were sold. His account of the sale of his mother and her six children (his father had already been sold and sent down South) is very touching."—*The Methodist,* Nov. 10th, 1876.

Crown 8vo, Fancy Boards, 1s. 6d.; in Handsome Embossed Cloth, Gilt Edges, 2s. 6d.

Order of any Bookseller, or direct from the Office, 89, Farringdon St., London, E.C

JUST OUT.

Order of any Bookseller or direct from the Office, 89, FARRINGDON
STREET, LONDON, E.C.

A VOLUME OF THRILLING INTEREST.

D. L. MOODY'S

"ARROWS AND *In Handsome Embossed Cloth, Gilt Edges,* 2s. 6d.

Crown 8vo, Fancy Boards,
1s. 6d. ANECDOTES."

BY JOHN LOBB,

Managing Editor of the "Christian Age."

*We gratefully record the hearty reception of this volume by the Christian
Public, and the flattering notices of our work by the Press, which have rendered
a new edition necessary within one month. We select the following*

OPINIONS OF THE PRESS.

"Some of these illustrations are original, and others have been borrowed from
well known sources and modified, we had almost said *Moody-fied.* Mr. Moody
never scrupled to declare that whatever he found that was good he appropriated,
and he was quite right in so doing. Now that Mr. Lobb has picked out the
plums from the pudding we see some of our own among them, and are glad
they were so well used ; but we see a great many of Mr. Moody's own growth,
which the ministers of the gospel must take care to preserve for future use.
This is a wise selection of pithy bits and live stories, such as wake men up, and
keep them awake too. God be thanked that Moody and Sankey ever came
among our churches ; it is well to gather up the fragments which remain after the
feast."—C. H. SPURGEON in *Sword and Trowel,* November, 1876.

"Most of the 'Anecdotes' in this volume undoubtedly bear the impress of
the evangelist who was lately amongst us. Any one familiar with his style will
recognise at a glance the short pointed sentences of concrete Saxon, with his
peculiarly natural and picturesque colouring. And in the light of all the
spurious counterfeits of Mr. Moody's style which have been published, one feels
grateful to the present editor for preserving the *aroma* of the original. If the
work was to be done, it was right that it should be done well, and, on the whole,
this is certainly well done. It would have been difficult to have done the work
much better than Mr. Lobb, to whom it has evidently been a labour of love."—
The Christian.

"'The religious movement conducted by Messrs. Moody and Sankey in the
chief cities of Great Britain and Ireland, during the years 1873—1875, in many
respects stands unparalleled in the history of revivals, and their visit will long
be held in grateful and loving remembrance by thousands.' The object in this
volume has been to collect the anecdotes and pointed sayings of Mr. Moody's,
as to stimulate Christian workers, and to assist in bringing home to those
h whom they come in contact the truths of the Gospel. The story of the

"Uncle Tom's Story of His Life."

AN

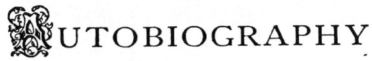UTOBIOGRAPHY

OF THE

REV. JOSIAH HENSON

(MRS. HARRIET BEECHER STOWE'S "UNCLE TOM").

From 1789 *to* 1876.

WITH A PREFACE

By MRS. HARRIET BEECHER STOWE,

AND AN

Introductory Note

By GEORGE STURGE, AND S. MORLEY, ESQ., M.P.

EDITED BY JOHN LOBB,

Managing Editor of the "Christian Age," Editor of D. L. Moody's "Arrows and Anecdotes" and "The Story of the Great Revival."

SIXTEENTH THOUSAND.

LONDON:
"CHRISTIAN AGE" OFFICE, 89, FARRINGDON STREET.
1876.

MRS. HARRIET BEECHER STOWE.

See page 212

PREFACE.

THE numerous friends of the author of this work will need no greater recommendation than his name to make it welcome. Among all the singular and interesting records to which the institution of American slavery has given rise, we know of none more striking, more characteristic and instructive, than that of Josiah Henson.

Born a slave—a slave in effect in a heathen land—and under a heathen master, he grew up without Christian light or knowledge, and like the Gentiles spoken of by St. Paul, "without the law did by nature the things that are written in the law." One sermon, one offer of salvation by Christ, was sufficient for him, as for the Ethiopian eunuch, to make him at once a believer from the heart and a preacher of Jesus.

To the great Christian doctrine of forgiveness of enemies and the returning of good for evil, he was by God's grace made a faithful witness, under circumstances that try men's souls and make us all who read it say, "Lead us not into such temptation." We earnestly commend this portion of his narrative to those who, under much smaller temptations, think themselves entitled to render evil for evil.

74385

The African race appear as yet to have been companions only of the sufferings of Christ.   In the melancholy scene of His death—while Europe in the person of the Roman delivered Him unto death, and Asia in the person of the Jew clamoured for His execution—Africa was represented in the person of Simon the Cyrenean, who came patiently bearing after Him the load of the cross; and ever since then poor Africa has been toiling on, bearing the weary cross of contempt and oppression after Jesus.   But they who suffer with Him shall also reign; and when the unwritten annals of slavery shall appear in the judgment, many Simons who have gone meekly bearing their cross after Jesus to unknown graves, shall rise to thrones and crowns!   Verily a day shall come when He shall appear for these His hidden ones, and then " many that are last shall be first, and the first shall be last."

HARRIET BEECHER STOWE.

Andover, Mass.

INTRODUCTORY NOTE.

By George Sturge, and S. Morley, Esq., M.P.

ON Rev. J. Henson's visit to England, Samuel Morley, Esq., M.P., and George Sturge, kindly undertook to be the treasurers of the fund to liquidate the claims of his mortgagees.

In response to our request for a few words intro-
ductory to "Uncle Tom's Life," we have the following from GEORGE STURGE.   "My knowledge of
Josiah Henson dates from his visit to this country
twenty-five years ago, when my late brother Thomas
Sturge, with other friends of the negro race, helped
to establish 'The Dawn Institute for the Education
of Coloured People in Canada.'   I regard Josiah
Henson in many respects as a remarkable man.
When I contemplate his unselfish efforts (at great
risk to himself) to rescue his brethren in slavery,
after he had obtained his own liberty, and his
labours as a free man to educate and enlighten them,
I consider that there are few men now living who
have done so much for the negro race.   When
it is remembered, too, that he was a slave for
forty-two years, his life affords an encouraging
example of what may be done, even by one who has
laboured ,under the greatest disadvantages, who
is earnestly desirous to benefit his race.   His
Christian simplicity, and the absence of all bitter
feeling towards those who have oppressed him, will
have commended him to all who have made his
acquaintance.   The life of 'Uncle Tom,' now extended in its records to the present date, will be
found by its readers to possess deep interest, and
will doubtless be favourably received. On submitting
these observations to SAMUEL MORLEY, his remark
was, 'I THOROUGHLY AGREE WITH THEM.'"

Sydenham, Oct. 1876.

CONTENTS.

MRS. H. BEECHER STOWE'S "UNCLE TOM."

CHAPTER I.

MY BIRTH AND CHILDHOOD.

EARLIEST MEMORIES.—BORN IN MARYLAND.—MY FATHER'S FIGHT
WITH AN OVERSEER.—ONE HUNDRED STRIPES AND HIS EAR CUT
OFF.—THROWS AWAY HIS BANJO AND BECOMES MOROSE.—SOLD
SOUTH.

THE story of my life, which I am about to record,
is one full of striking incident. Keener pangs,
deeper joys, more singular vicissitudes, few have
been led in God's providence to experience. As I
look back on it through the vista of more than
eighty years, and scene after scene rises before me,
an ever fresh wonder fills my mind. I delight to
recall it. I dwell on it as did the Jews on the mar-
vellous history of their rescue from the bondage of
Egypt. Time has touched with its mellowing fingers its sterner features. The sufferings of the past
are now like a dream, and the enduring lessons left
behind, make me to praise God that my soul has been

B

tempered by Him in so fiery a furnace and under such heavy blows.

I was born June 15th, 1789, in Charles county, Maryland, on a farm belonging to Mr. Francis Newman, about a mile from Port Tobacco. My mother was a slave of Dr. Josiah McPherson, but hired to Mr. Newman, to whom my father belonged. The only incident I can remember which occurred while my mother continued on Mr. Newman's farm, was the appearance one day of my father with his head bloody and his back lacerated. He was beside himself with mingled rage and suffering. The overseer had brutally assaulted my mother, when my father sprang upon him like a tiger. In a moment the overseer was down, and, mastered by rage, my father would have killed him but for the entreaties of my mother, and the overseer's own promise that nothing should ever be said of the matter. The promise was kept—like most promises of the cowardly and debased—as long as the danger lasted.

The laws of slave states provide means and opportunities for revenge so ample, that miscreants like him never fail to improve them. "A nigger has struck a white man;" that is enough to set a whole county on fire; no question is asked about the provocation. The authorities were soon in pursuit of my father. The penalty was one hundred lashes on the bare back, and to have the right ear nailed to the whipping-post, and then severed from the body. For a time my father kept out of the way, hiding in the woods, and at night venturing into some cabin in search of food. But at length the strict watch set baffled all his efforts. His supplies cut off, he was fairly starved out, and compelled by hunger to come back and give himself up.

The day for the execution of the penalty was appointed. The negroes from the neighbouring plantations were summoned to witness the scene. A powerful blacksmith named Hewes laid on the stripes. Fifty were given, during which the cries of my father might be heard a mile, and then a pause ensued. True, he had struck a white man, but as valuable property he must not be damaged. Judicious men felt his pulse. Oh! he could stand the whole. Again and again the thong fell on his lacerated back. His cries grew fainter and fainter, till a feeble groan was the only response to the final blows. His head was then thrust against the post, and his right ear fastened to it with a tack; a swift pass of a knife, and the bleeding member was left sticking to the place. Then came a hurra from the degraded crowd, and the exclamation, " That's what he's got for striking a white man."

In the estimation of the illiterate, besotted poor whites who constituted the witnesses of such scenes in Charles county, Maryland, the man who did not feel rage enough at hearing of " a nigger " striking a white, to be ready to burn him alive, was only fit to be lynched out of the neighbourhood.

Previous to this affair, my father, from all I can learn, had been a good-humoured and light-hearted man, the ringleader in all fun at corn-huskings and Christmas buffoonery. His banjo was the life of the farm, and all night long at a merry-making would he play on it while the other negroes danced. But from this hour he became utterly changed. Sullen, morose, and dogged, nothing could be done with him. The milk of human kindness in his heart was turned to gall. He brooded over his wrongs. No fear or threats of being sold to the far south—the greatest of all terrors to the Maryland slave—would render him tractable. So off he was sent to Alabama. What was his after-fate neither my mother nor I have ever learned ; the great day will reveal all. This was the first chapter in my history.

CHAPTER II.

MY FIRST GREAT TRIAL.

ORIGIN OF MY NAME.—A KIND MASTER.—HE IS DROWNED.—MY MOTHER'S PRAYERS.—A SLAVE AUCTION.—TORN FROM MY MOTHER.—SEVERE SICKNESS.—A CRUEL MASTER.—SOLD AGAIN AND RESTORED TO MY MOTHER.

AFTER the sale of my father by Newman, Dr. McPherson would no longer hire out my mother to him. She returned, accordingly, to his estate. He was far kinder to his slaves than the planters generally were, never suffering them to be struck by any one. He was a man of good, kind impulses, liberal, jovial, hearty. No degree of arbitrary power could ever lead him to cruelty. As the first negro child ever born to him, I was his especial pet. He gave me his own Christian name, Josiah, and with that he also gave me my last name, Henson, after an uncle of his, who was an officer in the revolutionary war. A bright spot in my childhood was my residence with him—bright, but, alas! fleeting. Events were rapidly maturing which were to change the whole aspect of my life. The kind doctor was not exempt from that failing which too often besets easy, social natures in a dissipated community. He could not restrain his convivial propensities. Although he maintained a high reputation for goodness of heart and an almost saint-like benevolence, the habit of intemperance steadily gained ground, and finally occasioned his death. Two negroes on the plantation found him one morning lying dead in the middle of a narrow stream, not a foot in depth. He had been away the night previous at a social party, and when returning home had fallen from his horse, probably, and being too intoxicated to stagger through the stream, fell and was drowned. " There's the place where massa got drownded at; " how well I remember having it pointed out to me in those very words.

For two or three years my mother and her young family of six children had resided on the doctor's estate, and we had been in the main very happy. She was a good mother to us, a woman of deep piety, anxious above all things to touch our hearts with a sense of religion. How or where she acquired her knowledge of God, or her acquaintance with the Lord's Prayer, which she so frequently taught us to repeat, I am unable to say. I remember seeing her often on her knees, and hearing her pray by repeating constant ejaculations, and short phrases which were within my infant comprehension, and have remained in my memory to this hour.

Our term of happy union as one family was now, alas! at an end. The doctor's death was a great calamity to us, for the estate and the slaves were to be sold and the proceeds divided among the heirs. The first sad announcement that the sale was to be ; the knowledge that all ties of the past were to be sundered ; the frantic terror at the idea of being sent "down south;" the almost certainty that one member of a family will be torn from another; the anxious scanning of purchasers' faces; the agony at parting, often for ever, with husband, wife, child—these must be seen and felt to be fully understood. Young as I was then, the iron entered into my soul. The remembrance of the breaking up of McPherson's estate is photographed in its minutest features in my mind. The crowd collected round the stand, the huddling group of negroes, the examination of muscle, teeth, the exhibition of agility, the look of the auctioneer, the agony of my mother—I can shut my eyes and see them all.

My brothers and sisters were bid off first, and one by one, while my mother, paralysed by grief, held me by the hand. Her turn came, and she was bought by Isaac Riley, of Montgomery county. Then I was offered to the assembled purchasers. My mother, half-distracted with the thought of parting for ever from all her children, pushed through the crowd, while the bidding for me was going on, to the spot where Riley was standing. She fell at his feet, and clung to his knees, entreating him in tones that a mother only could command, to buy her *baby* as well as herself, and spare to her one, at least, of her little ones. Will it, can it be believed that this man, thus appealed to, was capable not merely of turning a deaf ear to her supplication, but of disengaging himself from her with such violent blows and kicks, as to reduce her to the necessity of creeping out of his reach, and mingling the groan of bodily suffering with the sob of a breaking heart? As she crawled away from the brutal man, I heard her sob out, "Oh, Lord Jesus, how long, how long shall I suffer this way?" I must have been then between five and six years old.

I was bought by a stranger named Robb, and truly a robber he was to me. He took me to his home, about forty miles distant, and put me into his negro quarters with about forty others, of all ages, colours, and conditions, all strangers to me. Of course nobody cared for me. The slaves were brutalised by this degradation, and had no sympathy for me. I soon fell sick, and lay for some days almost dead on the ground. Sometimes a slave would give me a piece of corn-bread, or a bit of herring. Finally I became so feeble that I could not move. This, however, was fortunate for me; for in the course of a few weeks, Robb met Riley, who had bought my mother, and offered to sell me to him cheap. Riley said he was afraid "the little nigger would die;" but he agreed, finally, to pay a small sum for me in horse-shoeing if I lived, and nothing if I died. Robb was a tavern-keeper, and owned a line of stages with the horses, and lived near Montgomery Court House; Riley carried on blacksmithing about five miles from that place. This clenched the bargain, and I was soon sent to my mother. A blessed change it was. I had been lying on a lot of rags, thrown on a dirt floor. All day long I had been left alone, crying for water, crying for mother; the slaves, who left at daylight, when they returned cared nothing for me. Now, I was once more with my best friend on earth, and under her care; destitute as she was of the proper means of nursing me, I recovered my health, and grew to be an uncommonly vigorous boy and man.

I faithfully served Riley for many years. He was coarse and vulgar in his habits, and unprincipled and cruel in his general deportment. His slaves had little opportunity for relaxation from wearying labour, were supplied with the scantiest means of sustaining their toil by necessary food, and had no security for personal rights. When such a master is a tyrant, the slaves often become cringing, treacherous, false, and thieving. Riley and his slaves were no exception to the general rule, but might be cited as apt illustrations of the nature of the relation.

CHAPTER III.

MY BOYHOOD AND YOUTH.

EARLY EMPLOYMENT.—SLAVE-LIFE.—FOOD, LODGING, CLOTHING.—
AMUSEMENTS.—GLEAMS OF SUNSHINE.—MY KNIGHT-ERRANTRY.
—BECOME AN OVERSEER AND GENERAL SUPERINTENDENT.

My earliest employments were, to carry buckets of water to the men at work, and to hold a horse-plough, used for weeding between the rows of corn. As I grew older and taller, I was entrusted with the care of master's saddle-horse. Then a hoe was put into my hands, and I was soon required to do the day's work of a man; and it was not long before I could do it, at least as well as my associates in misery.

A description of the everyday life of a slave on a southern plantation illustrates the character and habits of the slave and the slaveholder, created and perpetuated by their relative position. The principal food of those upon my master's plantation consisted of corn-meal, and salt herrings; to which was added in summer a little buttermilk, and the few vegetables which each might raise for himself and his family, on the little piece of ground which was assigned to him for the purpose, called a truck-patch.

In ordinary times we had two regular meals in a

day: breakfast at twelve o'clock, after labouring from daylight, and supper when the work of the remainder of the day was over. In harvest season we had three. Our dress was of tow-cloth; for the children, nothing but a shirt; for the older ones a pair of pantaloons or a gown in addition, according to the sex. Besides these, in the winter a round jacket or overcoat, a wool-hat once in two or three years, for the males, and a pair of coarse shoes once a year.

We lodged in log huts, and on the bare ground. Wooden floors were an unknown luxury. In a single room were huddled, like cattle, ten or a dozen persons, men, women, and children. All ideas of refinement and decency were, of course, out of the question. We had neither bedsteads, nor furniture of any description. Our beds were collections of straw and old rags, thrown down in the corners and boxed in with boards; a single blanket the only covering. Our favourite way of sleeping, however, was on a plank, our heads raised on an old jacket and our feet toasting before the smouldering fire. The wind whistled and the rain and snow blew in through the cracks, and the damp earth soaked in the moisture till the floor was miry as a pig-sty. Such were our houses. In these wretched hovels were we penned at night, and fed by day; here were the children born and the sick—neglected.

Notwithstanding this system of management I grew to be a robust and vigorous lad. At fifteen years of age there were few who could compete with me in work or sport. I was as lively as a

young buck, and running over with animal spirits.
I could run faster, wrestle better, and jump higher
than anybody about me, and at an evening shake-
down in our own or a neighbour's kitchen, my feet
became absolutely invisible from the rate at which
they moved.   All this caused my master and my
fellow-slaves to look upon me as a wonderfully smart
fellow, and prophecy the great things I should do
when I became a man.   My vanity became vastly
inflamed, and 1 fully coincided in their opinion.
Julius Cæsar never aspired and plotted for the im-
perial crown more ambitiously than did I to out-hoe,
out-reap, out-husk, out-dance, out-strip every com-
petitor ; and from all I can learn he never enjoyed
his triumph half as much.   One word of commendation from the petty despot who ruled over us
would set me up for a month.

God be praised, that, however hedged in by circumstances, the joyful exuberance of youth will
bound at times over them all.   Ours is a light-
hearted race.   The sternest and most covetous
master cannot frighten or whip the fun out of us ;
certainly old Riley never did out of me.   In those
days I had many a merry time, and would have had,
had I lived with nothing but moccasins and rattle-
snakes in Okafenoke swamp.   Slavery did its best to
make me wretched, but, along with memories of miry
cabins, frosted feet, weary toil under the blazing
sun, curses and blows, there flock in others, of
jolly Christmas times, dances before old massa's door
for the first drink of egg-nog, extra meat at holiday
times, midnight-visits to apple-orchards, broiling

stray chickens, and first-rate tricks to dodge work. The God who makes the lambs gambol, the kittens play, the birds sing, and the fish leap, gave me a light, merry, and joyous heart. True it was, that the fun and freedom of Christmas, at which time my master relaxed his front, was generally followed up by a portentous back-action, under which he drove and cursed worse than ever; still the fun and freedom were fixed facts; we had had them and he could not help it.

Besides these pleasant memories I have others of a deeper and richer kind. I early learned to employ my spirit of adventure for the benefit of my fellow-sufferers. The condition of the male slave is bad enough; but that of the female, often compelled to perform severe labour, sick or well, unpitied and unaided, is one that arouses the spirit of sympathy in every heart not dead to all feeling. The miseries which I saw many of the women suffer, often oppressed me with a load of sorrow. No *white* knight, rescuing a white fair lady from cruel oppression, ever felt the throbbing of a chivalrous heart more intensely than I, a *black* knight, did, when running down a chicken to hide it in an out-of-the-way place till dark, that I might be able then to carry it to some poor overworked black fair one, to whom it was at once food, luxury, and medicine. No Scotch borderer, levying black mail or sweeping off a drove of cattle, ever felt more assured of the justice of his act than I of mine, when I was driving a pig or a sheep a mile or two into the woods, to slaughter

for the good of those whom Riley was starving.   I
felt good, moral, heroic.

Was this wrong?   I can only say in reply, that,
at this distance of time, my conscience does not
reproach me for it.   Then I esteemed it among the
best of my deeds.   It was my training in the luxury
of doing good, in the divinity of a sympathetic heart,
in the righteousness of indignation against the cruel
and oppressive.   There and then was my soul made
conscious of all the chivalry of which my circumstances and condition in life admitted.   I love the
sentiment in its splendid environment of castles,
and tilts, and gallantry; but having fallen on other
times, I loved it also in the homely guise of Sambo
as Paladin, Dinah as an oppressed maiden, and old
Riley as grim oppressor.

By means of the influence thus acquired, the great
amount of work I performed upon the farm, and by
the detection of the knavery of the overseer, who
plundered his employer for more selfish ends, was
caught in the act and dismissed, I was promoted to
be superintendent of the farm-work, and managed
to raise more than double the crops, with more
cheerful and willing labour, than was ever seen on
the estate before.

I was now, practically, overseer.   My pride and
ambition had made me master of every kind of farm-
work.   But, like all ambition, its reward was in-
crease of burdens.   The crops of wheat, oats, barley,
potatoes, corn, tobacco, all had to be cared for by
me.   I was often compelled to start at midnight
with the waggon for the distant market, to drive on

through mud and rain till morning, sell the produce, reach home hungry and tired, and nine times out of ten, reap my sole reward in curses for not getting higher prices. My master was a fearful blasphemer. Clearly as he saw my profitableness to him, he was too much of a brute to reward me with kindness or even decent treatment. Previous to my attaining this important station, however, an incident occurred which produced so powerful an influence on my intellectual development, my character, condition, my religious culture, and in short, on my whole nature, body and soul, that it deserves especial notice and commemoration. This, however, requires another chapter.

CHAPTER IV.

MY CONVERSION.

MY PRAYING MOTHER.—A GOOD MAN.—HEAR A SERMON FOR THE FIRST TIME.—ITS EFFECT UPON ME.—PRAYER AND COMMUNION. —ITS FIRST FRUITS.

I REMEMBER being torn from a dear and affectionate mother; I saw her tears and heard her groans; I remember all the particulars. From a little boy up I have remembered my mother; I remember what the prayers of my dear mother were; I have heard her pray for me; for she was a good Christian woman before I was born; and I thank God that I was born of a good Christian mother, a mother whose prayers fell on my ear. Of all earthly blessings there is none can approach to a good mother. I remember her entreaties; I remember her prayers to God for me. Blessed is the child, the son or daughter, that has the prayers of a mother. I remember well the feeling that those prayers wrought upon my heart, though I was but a boy.

My heart exults with gratitude when I mention the name of a good man who first taught me the blessedness of religion. His name was John McKenny. He lived at Georgetown, a few miles only from Riley's plantation; his business was that of a baker, and his character was that of an upright, benevolent Christian. He was noted especially for his detestation of slavery, and his resolute avoidance of the employment of slave-labour in his business. He would not even hire a slave, the price of whose toil must be paid to his master, but contented himself with the work of his own hands, and with such free labour as he could procure. His reputation was high, not only for this almost singular abstinence from what no one about him thought wrong, but for his general probity and excellence. This man occasionally served as a minister of the Gospel, and preached in a neighbourhood where preachers were somewhat rare at that period. One Sunday when he was to officiate in this way, at a place three or four miles distant, my mother urged me to ask master's permission to go and hear him. I had so often been beaten for making such a request that I refused to make it. My mother came to me and said: "Now, my son, I want you to go and ask master to let you go down and hear Mr. McKenny preach." I said to my mother: "I do not want to go; I am afraid he will beat me." She said: "Go and ask him." I turned round, like many other boys, and said I would not go. She was standing against a rail; she dropped her head down and shed a tear. I stood and looked at her and was touched at her sorrow. I said: "I will go, mother." She said: "That is right." I went up to the house, and just before I got to the door, master saw my shadow. He turned round and asked what I wanted. I said: "I want to ask you if I can go to the meeting." "Where?" "Down at New-port Mill." "Who is going to preach?" "Mr. McKenny." "What do you want to hear him preach for?" Here I was in a difficulty; I did not know what I wanted to go for, and I told him so. "What good will it do for you?" Here I was at another point. "Who put that into your head?" There was another thing; I did not want to get my poor old mother into trouble. But she had always told me to tell the truth. So I answered: "My mother." "Ah," said he, "I thought it was your mother. I suppose she wants to have you spoilt. When will you come back?" "As soon as meeting is over." Well, I went to the meeting, I heard the preacher, but I could not see him. They would not let niggers go into the meeting. I went all round the house; I could hear him, and at last I got in front of the door. I saw him with his hands raised, looking up to heaven, and he said, with emphasis: "Jesus Christ, the Son of God, tasted death for every man; for the high, for the low, for the rich, for the poor, the bond, the free, the negro in his chains, the man in gold and diamonds." His heart was filled with the love of Christ, and by the power of the Spirit of God he preached a universal salvation through Jesus Christ. I stood and heard it. It touched my heart, and I cried out: "I wonder if Jesus Christ died for me." And then I wondered what could have induced Him to die for me. I was then eighteen years old, I had never heard a sermon, nor any conversation whatever, upon religious topics, except what I had heard from my mother, on the responsibility of all to a Supreme Being. This was Heb. ii. 9, the first text of the Bible to which I had ever listened, knowing it to be such. I have never forgotten it, and scarcely a day has passed since, in which I have not recalled it, and the sermon that was preached from it.

The divine character of Jesus Christ, His tender love for mankind, His forgiving spirit, His compassion for the outcast and despised, His cruel crucifixion and glorious ascension, were all depicted, and some of the points were dwelt on with great power; great, at least, to me, who then heard of these things for the first time in my life. Again and again did the preacher reiterate the words "*for every man.*" These glad tidings, this salvation, were not for the benefit of a select few only. They were for the slave as well as the master, the poor as well as the rich, for the persecuted, the distressed, the heavy-laden, the captive; even for me among the rest, a poor, despised, abused creature, deemed by others fit for nothing but unrequited toil—but mental and bodily degradation. Oh, the blessedness and sweetness of feeling that I was LOVED! I would have died that moment with joy, and I kept repeating to myself, "The compassionate Saviour about whom I have heard 'loves me,' 'He looks down in compassion from heaven on me,' 'He died to save my soul,' and 'He'll welcome me to the skies.'" I was transported with delicious joy. I seemed to see a glorious being, in a cloud of splendour, smiling down from on high

In sharp contrast with the experience I had felt of the contempt and brutality of my earthly master, I basked, as it were, in the benign smiles of this Heavenly Being. I thought, "He'll be my dear refuge —He'll wipe away all tears from my eyes." "Now I can bear all things; nothing will seem hard after this." I felt sure that if "Massa Riley" only knew Him, he would not live such a coarse, wicked, cruel life. Swallowed up in the beauty of the divine love, I "loved my enemies, and prayed for them that did despitefully use and entreat me."

Revolving the things which I had heard in my mind as I went home. I became so excited that I turned aside from the road into the woods, and prayed to God for light and for aid with an earnestness, which, however unenlightened, was at least sincere and heartfelt; and which the subsequent course of my life has led me to imagine was acceptable to Him who heareth prayer. At all events, I date my conversion, and my awakening to a new life—a consciousness of power and a destiny superior to anything I had before conceived of—from this day, so memorable to me. I used every means and opportunity of inquiry into religious matters; and so deep was my conviction of their superior importance to everything else, so clear my perception of my own faults, and so undoubting my observation of the darkness and sin that surrounded me, that I could not help talking much on these subjects with those about me; and it was not long before I began to pray with them, exhort them, and impart to the poor slaves those little glimmerings of light from another world, which had reached my own eye. In a few years I became quite an esteemed preacher among them, and I believe that, through the grace of God, I was useful to many.

I must return, however, for the present, to the course of my life in secular affairs, the facts of which it is my principal object to relate.

CHAPTER V.

MAIMED FOR LIFE.

TAKING CARE OF MY DRUNKEN MASTER.—HIS FIGHT WITH AN
OVERSEER.—RESCUE HIM.—AM TERRIBLY BEATEN BY THE OVER-
SEER.—MY MASTER SEEKS REDRESS AT LAW, BUT FAILS.—
SUFFERINGS THEN AND SINCE.—RETAIN MY POST AS SUPERIN-
TENDENT.

THE difference between the manner in which it
was designed that all men should regard one
another as children of the same Father, and the
manner in which men of different colour actually
treated each other, is well exemplified by an incident
that happened to me within a year or two from this
period; that is, when I was nineteen or twenty years
old. My master's habits were such as were common
enough among the dissipated planters of the neighbourhood; and one of their frequent practices was
to assemble on Saturday or Sunday, which were
their holidays, and gamble, run horses, or fight
game-cocks, discuss politics, and drink whisky and
brandy-and-water all day long. Perfectly aware
that they would not be able to find their own way
home at night, each one ordered his body-servant
to come after him and help him home. I was chosen
for this confidential duty by my master; and many
were the times I have held him on his horse, when he

could not hold himself in the saddle, and walked by his side in darkness and mud from the tavern to his house. Quarrels and brawls of the most violent description were frequent consequences of these meetings; and whenever they became especially dangerous, and glasses were thrown, dirks drawn, and pistols fired, it was the duty of the slaves to rush in, and each one drag his master from the fight, and carry him home. To tell the truth, this was a part of my business for which I felt no reluctance. I was young, remarkably athletic and self-relying, and in such affrays I carried it with a high hand, and would elbow my way among the whites,—whom it would have been almost death for me to strike,—seize my master and drag him out, mount him on his horse, or crowd him into his buggy, with the ease with which I would handle a bag of corn. I knew that I was doing for him what he could not do for himself, showing my superiority to others, and acquiring their respect in some degree, at the same time.

On one of these occasions my master got into a quarrel with his brother's overseer, Bryce Litton. All present sided with Litton against him, and soon there was a general row. I was sitting, at the time, out on the front steps of the tavern, and, hearing the scuffle, rushed in to look after my charge. My master, a stout man and a terrible bruiser, could generally hold his own in an ordinary general fight, and clear a handsome space around him; but now he was cornered, and a dozen were striking at him with fists, crockery, chairs, and anything that came handy.

The moment he saw me, he hallooed, "That's it, Sie! pitch in! show me fair play." It was a rough business, and I went in roughly, shoving, tripping, and doing my best for the rescue. With infinite trouble, and many a bruise on my own head and shoulders, I at length got him out of the room. He was crazy with drink and rage, and struggled hard with me to get back and renew the fight. But I managed to force him into his waggon, jump in, and drive off.

By ill-luck, in the height of the scuffle, Bryce Litton got a severe fall. Whether the whisky he had drunk, or a chance-shove from me, was the cause, I am unable to say. He, however, attributed it to me, and treasured up his vengeance for the first favourable opportunity. The opportunity soon came.

About a week afterwards, I was sent by my master to a place a few miles distant, on horseback, with some letters. I took a short cut through a lane, separated by gates from the high road, and bounded by a fence on each side. This lane passed through a part of the farm owned by my master's brother, and his overseer was in the adjoining field, with three negroes, when I went by. On my return, half an hour afterwards, the overseer was sitting on the fence, but I could see nothing of the black fellows. I rode on, utterly unsuspicious of any trouble; but as I approached, he jumped off the fence, and at the same moment two of the negroes sprang up from under the bushes where they had been concealed, and stood with him immediately in front of me, while the third sprang over the fence just behind me. I was thus enclosed between what I could no longer doubt were hostile forces. The overseer seized my horse's bridle and ordered me to alight, in the usual elegant phraseology addressed by such men to slaves. I asked what I was to alight for. "To take the worst flogging you ever had in your life, you black scoundrel." He added many oaths that I will not repeat. "But what am I to be flogged for, Mr. L.?" I asked. "Not a word," said he, "but 'light at once, and take off your jacket." I saw there was nothing else to be done, and slipped off the horse on the opposite side from him. "Now take off your shirt," cried he; and as I demurred at this he lifted a stick he had in his hand to strike me, but so suddenly and violently that he frightened the horse, which broke away from him and ran home. I was thus left without means of escape to sustain the attacks of four men as well as I might. In avoiding Mr. L.'s blow, I had accidentally got into a corner of the fence where I could not be approached except in front. The overseer called upon the negroes to seize me; but they, knowing something of my physical power, were slow to obey. At length they did their best, and as they brought themselves within my reach I knocked them down successively; and I gave one of them, who tried to trip up my feet, when he was down, a kick with my heavy shoe, which knocked out several teeth, and sent him howling away.

Meanwhile Bryce Litton beat my head with a stick, not heavy enough to knock me down, but it drew blood freely. He shouted all the while, "Won't you give up! won't you give up!" adding oath after oath. Exasperated at my defence, he suddenly seized a heavy fence-rail and rushed at me with rage. The ponderous blow fell; I lifted my arm to ward it off, the bone cracked like a pipe-stem, and I fell headlong to the ground. Repeated blows then rained on my back till both shoulder-blades were broken, and the blood gushed copiously from my mouth. In vain the negroes interposed. "Didn't you see the nigger strike me?" Of course they must say "Yes," although the lying coward had avoided close quarters, and fought with his stick alone. At length, his vengeance satisfied, he desisted, telling me "to remember what it was to strike a white man."

Meanwhile an alarm had been raised at the house by the return of the horse without his rider, and my master started off with a small party to learn what the trouble was. When he first saw me he swore with rage. "You've been fighting, you mean nigger!" I told him Bryce Litton had been beating me, because he said I shoved him the other night at the tavern, when they had a fuss. Seeing how muc I was injured, he became still more fearfully mad; and after having me carried home, mounted his horse and rode over to Montgomery Court House to enter a complaint. Little good came of it. Litton swore that when he spoke to me in the lane I "sassed" him, jumped off my horse, attacked him, and would have killed him but for the help of his negroes. Of course no negro's testimony was admitted against a white man, and he was acquitted. My master was obliged to pay all the costs of court; and although

he had the satisfaction of calling Litton a liar and
scoundrel, and giving him a tremendous bruising,
still even this partial compensation was rendered less
gratifying by what followed, which was a suit for
damages and a heavy fine.

My sufferings after this cruel treatment were
intense. Besides my broken arm and the wounds
on my head, I could feel and hear the pieces of my
shoulder-blades grate against each other with every
breath. No physician or surgeon was called to dress
my wounds, and I never knew one to be called on
Riley's estate on any occasion whatever. " A nigger
will get well anyway," was a fixed principle of faith,
and facts seemed to justify it. The robust, physical
health produced by a life of outdoor labour, made
our wounds heal with as little inflammation as they
do in the case of cattle. I was attended by my
master's sister, Miss Patty, as we called her, the
Esculapius of the plantation. She was a powerful,
big-boned woman, who flinched at no responsibility,
from wrenching out teeth to setting bones. I have
seen her go into the house and get a rifle to shoot a
furious ox that the negroes were in vain trying to
butcher. She splintered my arm and bound up my
back as well as she knew how. Alas! it was but
cobbler's work. From that day to this I have been
unable to raise my hands as high as my head. It
was five months before I could work at all, and the
first time I tried to plough, a hard knock of the
coulter against a stone shattered my shoulder-blades
again, and gave me even greater agony than at
first. And so I have gone through life maimed and
mutilated. Practice in time enabled me to perform

many of the farm labours with considerable effi-
ciency; but the free, vigorous play of the muscles of
my arm was gone for ever.

I retained my situation as overseer, together with
the especial favour of my master, who was pleased
with saving the expense of a large salary for a white
superintendent, and with the superior crops I was
able to raise for him. I will not deny that I used
his property more freely than he would have done
himself, in supplying his people with better food;
but if I cheated him in this way, in small matters,
it was unequivocally for his own benefit in more
important ones; and I accounted, with the strictest
honesty, for every dollar I received in the sale of the
property entrusted to me. Gradually the disposal of
everything raised on the farm,—the wheat, oats,
hay, fruit, butter, and whatever else there might be,
—was confided to me, as it was quite evident that I
could and did sell for better prices than any one else
he could employ, and he was quite incompetent to
attend to the business himself. For many years I
was his factotum, and supplied him with all his
means for all his purposes, whether they were good
or bad. I had no reason to think highly of his
moral character; but it was my duty to be faithful
to him in the position in which he placed me; and I
can boldly declare, before God and man, that I was
so. I forgave him the causeless blows and injuries
he had inflicted on me in childhood and youth, and
was proud of the favour he now showed me, and of
the character and reputation I had earned by strenu-
ous and persevering efforts.

CHAPTER VI

A RESPONSIBLE JOURNEY.

MY MARRIAGE.—MARRIAGE OF MY MASTER.—HIS RUIN.—COMES TO ME FOR AID.—A GREAT ENTERPRISE UNDERTAKEN.—LONG AND SUCCESSFUL JOURNEY.—INCIDENTS BY THE WAY.—STRUGGLE BETWEEN INCLINATION AND DUTY.—DUTY TRIUMPHANT.

WHEN I was about twenty-two years of age, I married a very efficient, and, for a slave, a very well-taught girl, belonging to a neighbouring family reputed to be pious and kind. I first met her at the religious meetings which I attended. She has borne me twelve children, seven of whom still survive and promise to be the comfort of my declining years.

For a considerable period, my occupations were to superintend the farming operations, and to sell the produce in the neighbouring markets of Washington and Georgetown. Many respectable people, yet living there, may possibly have some recollection of "Siah," or "Sie," (as they used to call me,) as their market-man; but if they have forgotten me, I remember them with an honest satisfaction.

At length my master, at the age of forty-five, married a young woman of eighteen, who had some little property, and more thrift. Her economy was remarkable, and she added no comfort to the establishment. She had a younger brother, Francis, to whom Riley was appointed guardian, and who used to complain of the meanness of the provision made for the household; he would often come to me, with tears in his eyes, to tell me he could not get enough to eat. I made him my friend for life, by sympathising with him and satisfying his appetite, by sharing with him the food I took care to provide for my own family. He is still living, and, I understand, one of the wealthiest men in Washington city.

After a time, however, continual dissipation was more than a match for domestic saving. My master fell into difficulty, and from difficulty into a lawsuit with a brother-in-law, who charged him with dishonesty in the management of property confided to him in trust. The lawsuit was protracted enough to cause his ruin of itself.

Harsh and tyrannical as my master had been, I really pitied him in his present distress. At times he was dreadfully dejected, at others, crazy with drink and rage. Day after day would he ride over to Montgomery Court House about his business, and every day his affairs grew more desperate. He would come into my cabin to tell me how things were going, but spent the time chiefly in lamenting his misfortunes and cursing his brother-in-law. I tried to comfort him as best I could. He had confidence in my fidelity and judgment, and partly through pride, partly through that divine spirit of love I had learned to worship in Jesus, I entered with interest into all his perplexities. The poor, drinking, furious, shiftless, moaning creature was utterly incapable of managing his affairs.

One night in the month of January, long after I had fallen asleep, he came into my cabin and waked me up. I thought it strange, but for a time he said nothing, and sat moodily warming himself at the fire. Then he began to groan and wring his hands. "Sick, massa?" said I. He made no reply, but kept on moaning. "Can't I help you any way, massa?" I spoke tenderly, for my heart was full of compassion at his wretched appearance. At last, collecting himself, he cried, " Oh, Sie! I'm ruined, ruined, ruined!" "How so, massa?" "They've got judgment against me, and in less than two weeks every nigger I've got will be put up and sold." Then he burst into a storm of curses at his brother-in-law. I sat silent, powerless to utter a word. Pity for him and terror at the anticipation of my own family's future fate filled my heart. "And now, Sie," he continued, "there's only one way I can save anything. You can do it; won't you, won't you?" In his distress he rose and actually threw his arms around me. Misery had levelled all distinctions. "If I can do it, massa, I will. What is it?" Without replying he went on, "Won't you, won't you? I raised you, Sie; I made you overseer; I know I have abused you, Sie, but I didn't mean it." Still he avoided telling me what he wanted. "Promise me you'll do it, boy." He seemed resolutely bent on having my promise first, well knowing from past experience, that what I agreed to do I spared no pains to accomplish. Solicited in this way,

with urgency and tears, by the man whom I had so
zealously served for over thirty years, and who now
seemed absolutely dependent upon his slave; im-
pelled, too, by the fear which he skilfully awakened,
that the sheriff would seize every one who belonged
to him, and that all would be separated, or perhaps
sold to go to Georgia, or Louisiana—an object of
perpetual dread to the slave of the more northern
States—I consented, and promised faithfully to do
all I could to save him from the fate impending over
him.

At last the proposition came. "I want you to
run away, Sie, to my brother Amos in Kentucky,
and take all the servants along with you." I could
not have been more startled had he asked me to go
to the moon. "Kentucky, massa? Kentucky? I
don't know the way." "Oh, it's easy enough for a
smart fellow like you to find it; I'll give you a pass
and tell you just what to do." Perceiving that I
hesitated, he endeavoured to frighten me by again
referring to the terrors of being sold and taken to
Georgia.

For two or three hours he continued to urge the
undertaking, appealing to my pride, my sympathies,
and my fears, and at last, appalling as it seemed, I
told him I would do my best. There were eighteen
negroes, besides my wife, two children, and myself
to transport nearly a thousand miles, through a
country about which I knew nothing, and in mid-
winter, for it was the month of February, 1825.
My master proposed to follow me in a few months,
and establish himself in Kentucky.

My mind once made up, I set earnestly about the
needful preparations. They were few and easily
made. A one-horse waggon, well-stocked with oats,
meal, and bacon, for our own and the horse's support, was soon made ready. My pride was aroused
in view of the importance of my responsibility, and
heart and soul I became identified with my master's
project of running off his negroes. The second
night after the scheme was formed, we were under
way. Fortunately for the success of the undertaking, these people had long been under my direction,
and were devotedly attached to me in return for the
many alleviations I had afforded to their miserable
condition, the comforts I had procured them, and
the consideration I had always manifested for them.
Under these circumstances, no difficulty arose from
want of submission to my authority. The dread of
being separated, and sold away down south, should
they remain on the old estate, united them as one
man, and kept them patient and alert.

We started from home about eleven o'clock at
night, and till the following noon made no permanent
halt. The men trudged on foot, the children were
put into the waggon, and now and then my wife
rode for a while. On we went through Alexandria,
Culpepper, Fauquier, Harper's Ferry, Cumberland,
over the mountains on the National Turnpike to
Wheeling. In all the taverns along the road there
were regular places for the droves of negroes who
were continually passing through the country
under the care of overseers. In these we lodged,
and our lodging constituted our only expense, for our

D

food we carried with us.   To all who asked questions
I showed my master's pass, authorising me to conduct his negroes to Kentucky, and often was the
encomium of "smart nigger" bestowed on me, to
my immense gratification.

At the places where we stopped for the night, we
often met negro-drivers with their droves, who were
almost uniformly kept chained to prevent them from
running away.   The inquiry was often propounded
to me by the drivers, "Whose niggers are those?"
On being informed, the next inquiry usually was,
"Where are they going?" "To Kentucky." "Who
drives them?"   "Well, I have charge of them,"
was my reply.   "What a smart nigger!" was the
usual exclamation, with an oath.   "Will your master
sell you?   Come in and stop with us."   In this way
I was often invited to pass the evening with them in
the bar-room; their negroes, in the meantime, lying
chained in the pen, while mine were scattered around
at liberty.

Arriving at Wheeling, in pursuance of the plan
laid down by my master, I sold the horse and
waggon, and purchased a large boat, called in that
region, a yawl.   Our mode of locomotion was now
decidedly more agreeable than tramping along day
after day at the rate we had kept up ever since
leaving home.   Very little labour at the oars was
necessary. The tide floated us steadily along, and we
had ample leisure to sleep and recruit our strength.

A new and unexpected trouble now assailed me.
On passing along the Ohio shore, we were repeatedly
told by persons conversing with us that we were no
longer slaves but free men, if we chose to be so.   At

Cincinnati, especially, crowds of coloured people gathered round us, and insisted on our remaining with them. They told us we were fools to think of going on and surrendering ourselves up to a new owner ; that now we could be our own masters, and put ourselves out of all reach of pursuit. I saw that the people under me were getting much excited. Divided counsels and signs of insubordination began to manifest themselves. I began, too, to feel my own resolution giving way. Freedom had ever been an object of my ambition, though no other means of obtaining it had occurred to me but purchasing myself. I had never dreamed of running away. I had a sentiment of honour on the subject. The duties of the slave to his master as appointed over him in the Lord, I had ever heard urged by ministers and religious men. Entrancing as the ideas were, that the coast was clear for a run for freedom, that I might liberate my companions, might carry off my wife and children, and some day own a house and land, and be no longer despised and abused, still my notions of right were against it. I had promised my master to take his property to Kentucky, and deposit it with his brother Amos. Pride, too, came in to confirm me. I had undertaken a great thing ; my vanity had been flattered all along the road by hearing myself praised ; I thought it would be a feather in my cap to carry it through thoroughly, and had often painted the scene in my imagination of the final surrender of my charge to Master Amos, and the immense admiration and respect with which he would regard me.

Under the influence of these impressions, and

seeing that the allurements of the crowd were producing a manifest effect, I sternly assumed the captain, and ordered the boat to be pushed off into the stream. A shower of curses followed me from the shore; but the negroes under me, accustomed to obey, and, alas! too degraded and ignorant of the advantages of liberty to know what they were forfeiting, offered no resistance to my command.

Often since that day has my soul been pierced with bitter anguish, at the thought of having been thus instrumental in consigning to the infernal bondage of slavery, so many of my fellow-beings. I have wrestled in prayer with God for forgiveness. Having experienced myself the sweetness of liberty, and knowing too well the after-misery of a number of these slaves, my infatuation has often seemed to me to have been the unpardonable sin. But I console myself with the thought that I acted according to my best light, though the light that was in me was darkness. Those were my days of ignorance. I knew not then the glory of free manhood, or that the title-deed of the slave-owner is robbery and outrage.

What advantages I may have personally lost by thus throwing away an opportunity of obtaining freedom! But the perception of my own strength of character, the feeling of integrity, the sentiment of high honour, I thus gained by obedience to what I believed right, are advantages which I prize. He that is faithful over a little, will be faithful over much. Before God I tried to do my best, and the error of judgment lies at the door of the degrading system under which I had been nurtured.

CHAPTER VII.

A NEW HOME.

BECOME A METHODIST PREACHER.—MY POOR COMPANIONS SOLD.—
MY AGONY.—SENT FOR AGAIN.—INTERVIEW WITH A KIND
METHODIST PREACHER.—VISIT FREE SOIL AND BEGIN MY
STRUGGLE FOR FREEDOM.

I ARRIVED at Davis county, Kentucky, about the
middle of April, 1825, and delivered myself and
my companions to my owner's brother, Mr. Amos
Riley, who had a large plantation with from eighty
to one hundred negroes. His house was situated about
five miles south of the Ohio River, and fifteen miles
above the Yellow Banks, on Big Blackfords Creek.
There I remained three years, and was employed
meantime on the farm, of which I had the general
management, in consequence of the recommendation
for ability and honesty which I brought with me
from Maryland. The situation was, in many respects, more comfortable than the one I had left.
The farm was larger and more fertile, and there was
a greater abundance of food, which is, of course,
one of the principal sources of the comfort of a slave,
debarred as he is from so many enjoyments which
other men can obtain. Sufficiency of food is an important item in any man's account of life; it is
tenfold more so in that of the slave, whose appetite

is always stimulated by his arduous labour, and whose mind is little occupied by thought on subjects of deeper interest.   My post of superintendent gave me some advantages, of which I did not fail to avail myself, particularly with regard to those religious privileges, which, since I first heard of Christ and Christianity, had greatly occupied my mind.   In Kentucky the opportunities of attending the preach-ing of whites, as well as of blacks, were more numerous; and partly by attending them, and the camp-meetings which occurred from time to time, and partly from studying carefully my own heart, and observing the developments of character around me, in all the stations of life which I could watch, I became better acquainted with those religious feel-ings which are deeply implanted in the breast of every human being, and learned by practice how best to arouse them, and keep them excited, how to stir up the callous and indifferent, and, in general, to produce some good religious impressions on the ignorant and thoughtless community by which I was surrounded.

No great amount of theological knowledge is re-quisite for the purpose.   If it had been, it is manifest enough that preaching never could have been my vocation; but I am persuaded that, speaking from the fulness of a heart deeply impressed with its own sinfulness and imperfection, and with the mercy of God, in Christ Jesus, my humble ministrations have not been entirely useless to those who have had less opportunity than myself to reflect upon these all-important subjects.   It is certain that I could not refrain from the endeavour to do what I saw others doing in this field; and I laboured at once to improve myself and those about me in the cultivation of the harvests which ripen only in eternity. I cannot but derive some satisfaction, too, from the proofs I have had that my services have been acceptable to those to whom they have been rendered. In the course of three years, from 1825 to 1828, I availed myself of all the opportunities of improvement which occurred, and was admitted as a preacher by a Quarterly Conference of the Methodist Episcopal Church.

In the spring of the year 1828, news arrived from my master that he was unable to induce his wife to accompany him to Kentucky, and that he must therefore remain where he was. He sent out an agent to sell all his slaves, except me and my family, and to carry back the proceeds to him. And now another of those heartrending scenes was to be witnessed, which had impressed itself so deeply on my childish soul. Husbands and wives, parents and children, were to be separated for ever. Affections, which are as strong in the African as in the European, were to be cruelly disregarded; and the iron selfishness generated by the hateful "institution," was to be exhibited in its most odious and naked deformity. I was exempted from a personal share in the dreadful calamity; but I could not see without the deepest grief, the agony of my associates. It was like that my own mother had once manifested, when I was separated from her for a time. I could not refrain from feeling the bitterest hatred of the system, and of those who sustained it. What else, indeed, could be

the feeling of a slave, liable at every moment of his
life to these frightful and unnecessary calamities,
which might be caused by the caprice, or the supposed
necessities of the slaveholders, and inflicted upon
him without sympathy or redress, under the sanction
of the laws which upheld the institution?

As I surveyed this scene, and listened to the
groans and outcries of my afflicted companions, my
eyes were opened, and I lamented that I had prevented them from availing themselves of the opportunity for acquiring freedom which offered itself at
Cincinnati. I had only thought of being faithful to
my master's interests, and nothing of the welfare of
the slaves. Oh! what would I not have given to
have had the chance offered once more! But now,
through me, were they doomed to wear out life
miserably in the hot and pestilential climate of the
far south. Death would have been welcome to me
in my agony. From that hour I saw through,
hated, and cursed the whole system of slavery. One
absorbing purpose occupied my soul—to gain freedom, self-assertion, and deliverance from the cruel
caprices and fortunes of dissolute tyrants. Once to
get away, with my wife and children, to some spot
where I could feel that they were indeed *mine*—
where no grasping master could stand between me
and them, as arbiter of their destiny—was a heaven
yearned after with insatiable longing. For it I stood
ready to pray, toil, dissemble, plot like a fox, and
fight like a tiger. All the noble instincts of my
soul, and all the ferocious passions of my animal
nature, were aroused and quickened into vigorous
action.

The object of my old master Riley in directing that I and my family should be exempted from the sale, was a desire on his part to get me back to Maryland, and employ me in his own service. His best farms had been taken away from him, and but a few tracts of poor land remained, which he cultivated with hired labour after I took his slaves, and month by month he grew poorer and more desperate. He had written to his brother Amos to give me a pass and let me travel back; but this his brother was reluctant to do, as I saved him the expense of an overseer, and he moreover was aware that no legal steps could be taken to force him to comply. I knew of all this, but dared not seem anxious to return, for fear of exciting suspicion.

In the course of the summer of 1828, a Methodist preacher, a most excellent white man, visited our neighbourhood, and I became acquainted with him. He was soon interested in me, and visited me frequently, and one day talked to me in a confidential manner about my position. He said, " You ought to be free. You have too much capacity to be confined to the limited and comparatively useless sphere of a slave, and though it must not be known that I have spoken to you on this subject, yet, if you will obtain Mr. Amos's consent to go to see your old master in Maryland, I will try and put you in a way by which I think you may succeed in buying yourself." He said this to me more than once; and as it was in harmony with all my aspirations and wishes, was flattering to my self-esteem, and gratified my impatience to bring matters to a direct issue, I now resolved to make the attempt to get the necessary leave. The autumn work was over, I was no longer needed in the fields, and a better chance would never offer itself. Still I dreaded to make the proposal. So much hung on it, such fond hopes were bound up with it, that I trembled for the result.

I opened the subject one Sunday morning while shaving Mr. Amos, and adroitly managed, by bringing the shaving brush close into his mouth whenever he was disposed to interrupt me, to "get a good say" first. Of course, I made no allusion to my plan of buying myself, but urged my request on the sole ground of a desire to see my old master. To my surprise, he made little objection. I had been faithful to him, and gained, in his rude way of showing it, his regard. Long before spring I would be back again. He even told me I had earned such a privilege.

The certificate he gave me, allowed me to pass and repass between Kentucky and Maryland as servant of Amos Riley. Furnished with this, and with a letter of recommendation from my Methodist friend to a brother preacher in Cincinnati, I started about the middle of September, 1828, for the east.

A new era in my history now opened upon me. A letter I carried with me to a kind-hearted man in Cincinnati, procured me a number of invaluable friends, who entered heart and soul into my plans. They procured me an opportunity to preach in two or three of the pulpits of the city, and I made my appeal with that eloquence which spontaneously breaks forth from a breast all alive and fanned into a glow by an inspiring project. Contact with those who were free themselves, and a proud sense of exultation in taking my destiny into my own hands, gave me the sacred "gift of tongues." I was pleading an issue of life and death, of heaven and hell, and such as heard me felt this in their hearts. In three or four days I left the city with no less a sum than one hundred and sixty dollars in my pockets, and with a soul jubilant with thanksgiving, and high in hope, directed my steps towards Chillicothe, to attend the session of the Ohio Conference of the Methodist Episcopal Church. My kind friend accompanied me, and, by his influence and exertions, still further success attended me.

By his advice, I then purchased a decent suit of clothes and an excellent horse, and travelled from town to town, preaching as I went. Everywhere I met with kindness. The contrast between the respect with which I was treated and the ordinary abuse of plantation life, gratified me in the extreme, as it must any one who has within him one spark of personal dignity as a man. The sweet enjoyment of sympathy, moreover, and the hearty "God speed you, brother!" which accompanied every dollar I received, were to my long-starved heart a celestial repast, and angels' food. Liberty was a glorious hope in my mind; not as an escape from toil, for I rejoiced in toil when my heart was in it, but as the avenue to a sense of self-respect, to ennobling occupation, and to association with superior minds. Still, dear as was the thought of liberty, I still clung to my determination to gain it in one way only—by purchase. The cup of my affliction was not yet full enough to lead me to disregard all terms with my master.

CHAPTER VIII.

RETURN TO MARYLAND.

RECEPTION FROM MY OLD MASTER.—A SLAVE AGAIN.—APPEAL TO
AN OLD FRIEND.—BUY MY FREEDOM.—CHEATED AND BETRAYED.
—BACK TO KENTUCKY, AND A SLAVE AGAIN.

BEFORE I left Ohio and set my face towards Montgomery county, I was master of two hundred and seventy-five dollars, besides my horse and clothes. Proud of my success, I enjoyed the thought of showing myself once more in the place where I had been known simply as "Riley's head-nigger;" and it was with no little satisfaction that about Christmas I rode up to the old house.

My master gave me a boisterous reception, and expressed great delight at seeing me. "What have you been doing, Sie? you've turned into a regular black gentleman." My horse and dress sorely puzzled him, and I soon saw they irritated him. The clothes I wore were certainly better than his. Very soon the workings of that tyrannical hate with which the coarse and brutal, who have no inherent superiority, ever regard the least sign of equality in their dependents, were visible in his manner. His face seemed to say, "I'll take the gentleman out of you pretty soon." I gave him an account of my preaching which was consistent with the truth, and explained my appearance, but did not betray to him my principal purpose. He soon asked to see my pass, and when he found it authorised me to return to Kentucky, handed it to his wife, and desired her to put it into his desk. The manœuvre was cool and startling. I heard the old prison-gate clang, and the bolt shoot into the socket once more. But I said nothing, and resolved to manœuvre also.

After putting my horse in the stable I retired to the kitchen, where my master told me I was to sleep for the night. Oh, how different from my accommodations in the free States, for the last three months, was that crowded room, with its earth-floor, its filth and stench! I looked around me with a sensation of disgust. The negroes present were strangers to me. I found my mother had died during my absence, and every tie which had ever connected me with the place was broken. Full of gloomy reflections at my loneliness, and the poverty-stricken aspect of the whole farm, I sat down, and while my companions were snoring in unconsciousness, I kept awake, thinking how I could escape from the accursed spot. I knew of but one friend to whom I could appeal—"Master Frank," the brother of Riley's wife, before mentioned, who was now of age, and had established himself in business in Washington. I thought he would take an interest in me, for I had done much to lighten his sorrows when he was an abused and harshly-treated boy in the house. To him I resolved to go, and as soon as I thought it time to start, I saddled my horse and rode up to the house. It was early in the morning, and my master had already gone to the tavern on his usual business, when Mrs. Riley came out to look at my horse and equipments. "Where are you going, 'Siah?" was the natural question. I replied, "I am going to Washington, mistress, to see Mr. Frank, and I must take my pass with me, if you please." "Oh, everybody knows you here; you won't need your pass." "But I can't go to Washington without it. I may be met by some surly stranger, who will stop me and plague me, if he can't do anything worse." "Well, I'll get it for you," she answered; and glad I was to see her return with it in her hand, and to have her give it to me, while she little imagined its importance to my plan.

My reception by Master Frank was all I expected, as kind and hearty as possible. He was delighted at my appearance, and I immediately told him all my plans and hopes. He entered cordially into them, and expressed a strong sympathy for me. I found that he thoroughly detested Riley, whom he charged with having defrauded him of a large proportion of his property which he had held as guardian, though, as he was not at warfare with him, he readily agreed to negotiate for my freedom, and bring him to the most favourable terms. Accordingly, in a few days he rode over to the house, and had a long conversation with him on the subject of my emancipation. He disclosed to him the facts that I had got some money and *my pass*, and urged that I was a smart fellow, who was bent upon getting his freedom, and naa served the family faithfully for many years; that I had really paid for myself a hundred times

over, in the increased amount of produce I had raised
by my skill and influence; and that if he did not
take care, and accept a fair offer when I made it to
him, he would find some day that I had the means
to do without his help, and that he would see neither
me nor my money; that with my horse and my
pass I was pretty independent of him already, and
he had better make up his mind to do what was
really inevitable, and do it with a good grace. By
such arguments as these, Mr. Frank not only induced
him to think of the thing, but before long brought
him to an actual bargain, by which he agreed to
give me my manumission-papers for four hundred
and fifty dollars, of which three hundred and fifty
dollars were to be in cash, and the remainder in my
note. My money and my horse enabled me to pay
the cash at once, and thus my great hope seemed in
a fair way of being realised.

Some time was spent in the negotiation of this
affair, and it was not until the 9th of March, 1829,
that I received my manumission-papers in due form
of law. I prepared to start at once on my return to
Kentucky; and on the 10th, as I was getting ready,
in the morning, for my journey, my master accosted
me in the most friendly manner, and entered into
conversation with me about my plans. He asked me
what I was going to do with my certificate of freedom; whether I was going to show it, if questioned
on the road. I told him, "Yes." "You'll be a fool
if you do," he rejoined. "Some slave-trader will
get hold of it, and tear it up, and you'll be thrown
into prison, sold for your jail-fees, and be in his

possession before any of your friends can help you. Don't show it at all. Your pass is enough. Let me enclose your papers for you under cover to my brother. Nobody will dare to break a seal, for that is a state-prison matter; and when you arrive in Kentucky you will have it with you all safe and sound."

For this friendly advice, as I thought it, I felt extremely grateful. Secure in my happiness, I cherished no suspicion of others. I accordingly permitted him to enclose my precious papers in an envelope composed of several wrappers, and after he had sealed it with three seals, and directed it to his brother in Davies county, Kentucky, he gave it to me, and I carefully stowed it in my carpet-bag. Leaving immediately for Wheeling, to which place I was obliged to travel on foot, I there took boat, and in due time reached my destination. I was arrested repeatedly on the way; but by insisting always on being carried before a magistrate, I succeeded in escaping all serious impediments by means of my pass, which was quite regular, and could not be set aside by any responsible authority.

The boat which took me down from Louisville, landed me about dark, and my walk of five miles brought me to the plantation at bedtime. I went directly to my own cabin, and found my wife and little ones well. Of course we had enough to communicate to each other. I soon found that I had something to learn as well as to tell. Letters had reached the "great house,"—as the master's was always called,—long before I arrived, telling them what I had been doing. The children of the family had eagerly communicated the good news to my wife —how I had been preaching, and raising money, and making a bargain for my freedom. It was not long before Charlotte began to question me, with much excitement, how I had raised the money. She evidently thought I had stolen it. Her opinion of my powers as a preacher was not exalted enough to permit her to believe I had gained it as I really did. I contrived, however, to quiet her fears on this score. "But how are you going to raise enough to pay the remainder of the thousand dollars?" "What thousand dollars?" "The thousand dollars you are to give for your freedom." Oh, how those words smote me! At once I suspected treachery. Again and again I questioned her as to what she had heard. She persisted in repeating the same story as the substance of my master's letters. Master Amos said I had paid three hundred and fifty dollars down, and when I had made up six hundred and fifty more I was to have my free papers. I now began to perceive the trick that had been played upon me, and to see the management by which Riley had contrived that the only evidence of my freedom should be kept from every eye but that of his brother Amos, who was requested to retain it until I had made up the balance I was reported to have agreed to pay. Indignation is a faint word to express my deep sense of such villainy. I was alternately beside myself with rage, and paralysed with despair. My dream of bliss was over. What could I do to set myself right? The only witness to the truth,

E

Master Frank, was a thousand miles away. I could neither write to him, nor get any one else to write. Every man about me who could write was a slaveholder. I dared not go before a magistrate with my papers, for fear I should be seized and sold down the river before anything could be done. I felt that every white man's hand was against me. "My God! my God! why hast Thou forsaken me?" was my bitter cry. One thing only seemed clear. My papers must never be surrendered to Master Amos. I told my wife I had not seen them since I left Louisville. They might be in my bag, or they might be lost. At all events I did not wish to look myself. If she found them there, and hid them away, out of my knowledge, it would be the best disposition to make of them.

The next morning, at the blowing of the horn, I went out to find Master Amos. I found him sitting on a stile, and as I drew near enough for him to recognise me, he shouted out a hearty welcome in his usual style. "Why, halloa, Sie! is that you? Got back, eh! I'm glad to see you! why, you're a regular black gentleman!" And he surveyed my dress with an appreciative grin. "Well, boy, how's your master? Isaac says you want to be free. Want to be free, eh! I think your master treats you pretty hard, though. Six hundred and fifty dollars don't come so easy in old Kentuck. How does he ever expect you to raise all that? It's too much, boy, it's too much." In the conversation that followed I found my wife was right. Riley had no idea of letting me off, and supposed I could never raise the six hundred and fifty dollars if his brother obtained possession of me.

Master Amos soon asked me if I had not a paper for him. I told him I had had one, but the last I saw of it was at Louisville, and now it was not in my bag, and I did not know what had become of it. He sent me back to the landing to see if it had been dropped on the way. Of course I did not find it. He made, however, little stir about it, for he had intentions of his own to keep me working for him, and regarded the whole as a trick of his brother's to get money out of me. All he said about the loss was, " Well, boy, bad luck happens to everybody, sometimes."

All this was very smooth and pleasant to a man who was in a frenzy of grief at the base and apparently irremediable trick that had been played upon him. I had supposed that I should soon be free to start out and gain the hundred dollars which would discharge my obligation to my master. But I perceived that I was to begin again with my old labours. It was useless to give expression to my feelings, and I went about my work with as quiet a mind as I could, resolved to trust in God, and never despair.

CHAPTER IX.

TAKEN SOUTH, AWAY FROM WIFE AND CHILDREN.

START FOR NEW ORLEANS.—STUDY NAVIGATION ON THE MISSISSIPPI. —THE CAPTAIN STRUCK BLIND.—FIND SOME OF MY OLD COMPANIONS.—THE LOWER DEPTHS.

THINGS went on in this way about a year. From time to time Master Amos joked me about the six hundred and fifty dollars, and said his brother kept writing to know why I did not send something. It was "diamond cut diamond" with the two brothers. Mr. Amos had no desire to play into the hands of Mr. Isaac. He was glad enough to secure my services to take care of his stock and his people.

One day my master suddenly informed me that his son Amos, a young man about twenty-one years of age, was going down the river to New Orleans, with a flat-boat loaded with produce from the farm, and that I was to go with him. He was to start the next day, and I was to accompany him and help him dispose of his cargo to the best advantage.

This intimation was enough. Though it was not distinctly stated, yet I well knew what was intended, and my heart sunk within me at the prospect of this fatal blight to all my long-cherished hopes. There was no alternative but death itself;

still I thought that there was hope as long as there was life, and I would not despair even yet. The expectation of my fate, however, produced the degree of misery nearest to that of despair, and it is in vain for me to attempt to describe the wretchedness I experienced as I made ready to go on board the flatboat. I had little preparation to make, to be sure; but there was one thing that seemed to me important. I asked my wife to sew my manumission-paper securely in a piece of cloth, and to sew that again round my person. I thought that its possession might be the means of saving me yet, and I would not neglect anything that offered the smallest chance of escape from the frightful servitude with which I was threatened.

The immediate cause of this movement on the part of Master Amos I never fully understood. It grew out of a frequent exchange of letters, which had been kept up between him and his brother in Maryland. Whether as a compromise between their rival claims it was agreed to sell me and divide the proceeds, or that Master Amos, in fear of my running away, had resolved to turn me into riches without wings, for his own profit, I never knew. The fact of his intention, however, was clear enough; and God knows it was a fearful blow.

My wife and children accompanied me to the landing, where I bade them an adieu which might be for life, and then stepped into the boat, manned by three white men, who had been hired for the trip. Mr. Amos and myself were the only other persons on board. The load consisted of beef-cattle, pigs, poultry, corn, whisky, and other articles which were to be sold as we dropped down the river, wherever they could be disposed of to the greatest advantage. It was a common trading-voyage to New Orleans, the interest of which consisted not in the incidents that occurred, not in storms, shipwreck, or external disaster of any sort ; but in the storm of passions contending within me, and the imminent risk of the shipwreck of my soul, which was impending over me nearly the whole period of the voyage. One circumstance, only, I will mention, illustrating, as other events in my life have often done, the counsel of the Saviour, "He that will be chief among you, let him be your servant."

We were all bound to take our turn at the helm, sometimes under direction of the captain, and sometimes on our own responsibility, as he could not be always awake. In the daytime there was less difficulty than at night, when it required some one who knew how to avoid sandbars and snags in the river ; the captain was the only person on board who had this knowledge. But whether by day or by night, as I was the only negro in the boat, I was compelled to stand at least three turns at the helm to any other person's one; so that, from being much with the captain, and frequently thrown upon my own exertions, I learned the art of steering and managing the boat far better than the rest. I watched the manœuvres necessary to shoot by a "sawyer," to land on a bank, avoid a snag, or a steamboat, in the rapid current of the Mississippi, till I could do it as well as the captain. After a while, he was attacked

by a disease of the eyes ; they became very much
inflamed and swollen. He was soon rendered totally
blind, and unable to perform his share of duty. I
was the person who could best take his place, and I
was in fact master of the boat from that time till
our arrival at New Orleans.

After the captain became blind, we were obliged
to lie by at night, as none of the rest of us had
been down the river before ; and it was necessary to
keep watch all night, to prevent depredations by the
negroes on shore, who used frequently to attack such
boats as ours, for the sake of the provisions on board.

On our way down the river we stopped at Vicksburg, and I got permission to visit a plantation a
few miles from the town, where some of my old
companions whom I had brought from Kentucky
were living. It was the saddest visit I ever made.
Four years in an unhealthy climate and under a hard
master had done the ordinary work of twenty. Their
cheeks were literally caved in with starvation and
disease. They described their daily life, which was to
toil half-naked in malarious marshes, under a burning,
maddening sun, exposed to poison of mosquitoes and
black gnats, and they said they looked forward to
death as their only deliverance. Some of them
fairly cried at seeing me there, and at the thought
of the fate which they felt awaited me. Their worst
fears of being sold down South had been more than
realised. I went away sick at heart, and to this day
the remembrance of that wretched group haunts me

CHAPTER X.

A TERRIBLE TEMPTATION.

ALL outward nature seemed to feed my gloomy
thoughts. I know not what most men see in
voyaging down the Mississippi. If gay and hopeful,
probably much of beauty and interest. If eager
merchants, probably a golden river, freighted with
the wealth of nations. I saw nothing but portents
of woe and despair. Wretched slave-pens; a smell
of stagnant waters; half-putrid carcases of horses
or·oxen floating along, covered with turkey-buzzards
and swarms of green flies,—these are the images
with which memory crowds my mind. My faith in
God utterly gave way. I could no longer pray or
trust. I thought He had abandoned me and cast me
off for ever. I looked not to Him for help. I saw
only the foul miasmas, the emaciated frames of my
negro companions; and in them saw the sure, swift,
loving intervention of the one unfailing friend of the
wretched,—death! Yes; death and the grave!
"There the wicked cease from troubling, and the
weary are at rest. There the prisoners rest together;
they hear not the voice of the oppressor." Two
years of this would kill me. I dwelt on the thought

with melancholy yet sweet satisfaction. Two years! and then I should be free. Free! ever my cherished hope, though not as I had thought it would come.

As I paced backwards and forwards on the deck, during my watch, I revolved in my mind many a painful and passionate thought. After all that I had done for Isaac and Amos Riley, after all the regard they had professed for me, such a return as this for my services, such an evidence of their utter disregard of my claims upon them, and the intense selfishness with which they were ready to sacrifice me, at any moment, to their supposed interest, turned my blood to gall, and changed me from a lively, and, I will say, a pleasant-tempered fellow, into a savage, morose, dangerous slave. I was going not at all as a lamb to the slaughter; but I felt myself becoming more ferocious every day; and as we approached the place where this iniquity was to be consummated, I became more and more agitated with an almost uncontrollable fury. I said to myself, " If this is to be my lot, I cannot survive it long. I am not so young as those whose wretched condition I have but just seen, and if it has brought them to such a condition, it will soon kill me. I am to be taken to a place and a condition where my life is to be shortened, as well as made more wretched. Why should I not prevent this wrong if I can, by shortening the lives of those who intend to accomplish such injustice? I can do the last easily enough. They have no suspicion of me, and they are at this moment under my control, and in my power. There are many ways in which I can dispatch them and escape; and I feel that I should be justified in availing myself of the first good opportunity." These thoughts did not flit across my mind's eye and then disappear, but they fashioned themselves into shapes which grew larger and seemed firmer every time they presented themselves ; at length my mind was made up to convert the phantom-shadows into a positive reality.

I resolved to kill my four companions, take what money there was in the boat, scuttle the craft, and escape to the north. It was a poor plan, maybe, and would very likely have failed ; but it was as well contrived, under the circumstances, as the plans of murderers usually are. Blinded by passion, and stung to madness as I was, I could not see any difficulty about it. One dark, rainy night, within a few days' sail of New Orleans, my hour seemed to have come. I was alone on the deck, Master Amos and the hands were all asleep below, and I crept down noiselessly, got hold of an axe, entered the cabin, and looking by the aid of the dim light there for my victims, my eyes fell upon Master Amos, who was nearest to me, my hand slid along the axe-handle, I raised it to strike the fatal blow,—when suddenly the thought came to me, "What! commit *murder !* and you a Christian ?" I had not called it murder before, but self-defence, to prevent others from murdering me. I thought it was justifiable, and even praiseworthy. All at once the truth burst upon me that it was a crime. I was going to kill a young man who had done nothing to injure me, but was only obeying the commands of his father. I was about to lose the fruit of all my efforts at self-improvement, the character I had acquired, and the peace of mind that had never deserted me. All this came upon me with a distinctness which almost made me think I heard it whispered in my ear; and I believe I even turned my head to listen. I shrunk back, laid down the axe, and thanked God, as I have done every day since, that I did not commit that murder.

My feelings were still agitated, but they were changed. I was filled with shame and remorse for the design I had entertained, and fearing that my companions would detect it in my face, or that a careless word would betray my guilty thoughts, I remained on deck all night, instead of rousing one of the men to relieve the watch, and nothing brought composure to my mind but the solemn resolution I then made, to resign myself to the will of God, and take with thankfulness, if I could, but with submission, at all events, whatever He might decide should be my lot. I reflected that if my life were reduced to a brief term, I should have less to suffer; that it was better to die with a Christian's hope, and a quiet conscience, than to live with the incessant recollection of a crime that would destroy the value of life, and under the weight of a secret that would crush out the satisfaction that might be expected from freedom and every other blessing.

It was long before I recovered my self-control and serenity. Yet I believe that no one but those to whom I have told the story myself, ever suspected me of having entertained such thoughts for a moment.

CHAPTER XI.

PROVIDENTIAL DELIVERANCE.

OFFERED FOR SALE.—EXAMINED BY PURCHASERS.—PLEAD WITH
MY YOUNG MASTER IN VAIN.—MAN'S EXTREMITY, GOD'S OPPOR-
TUNITY.—GOOD FOR EVIL.—RETURN NORTH.—MY INCREASED
VALUE.—RESOLVE TO BE A SLAVE NO LONGER.

IN a few days after this trying crisis in my life, we
arrived at New Orleans. The little that remained of our cargo was soon sold, the men were
discharged, and nothing was left but to dispose of
me, and break up the boat, and then Master Amos
intended to take passage on a steamboat, and go
home. There was no longer any disguise about the
disposition which was to be made of me. Master
Amos acknowledged that such were his instructions,
and he set about fulfilling them. Several planters
came to the boat to look at me; I was sent on some
hasty errand that they might see how I could run;
my points were canvassed as those of a horse would
have been; and, doubtless, some account of my
various faculties entered into the discussion of the
bargain, that my value as a domestic animal might
be enhanced. Master Amos had talked, with ap-
parent kindness, about getting me a good master who
would employ me as a coachman, or as a house-

servant; but as time passed on I could discern no particular effort of the kind.

In our intervals of leisure I tried every possible means to move his heart. With tears and groans I besought him not to sell me away from my wife and children. I dwelt on my past services to his father, and called to his remembrance a thousand things I had done for him personally. I told him about the wretched condition of the slaves I had seen near Vicksburg. Sometimes he would shed tears himself, and say he was sorry for me. But still I saw his purpose was unchanged. He now kept out of my way as much as possible, and forestalled every effort I made to talk with him. His conscience evidently troubled him. He knew he was doing a cruel and wicked thing, and wanted to escape from thinking about it. I followed him up hard, for I was supplicating for my life. I fell down and clung to his knees in entreaties. Sometimes when too closely pressed, he would curse and strike me. May God forgive him! And yet it was not all his fault; he was made so by the accursed relation of slave-master and slave. I was property,—not a man, not a father, not a husband. And the laws of property and self-interest, not of humanity and love, bore sway.

At length everything was wound up but this single affair. I was to be sold the next day, and Master Amos was to set off on his return in a steamboat at six o'clock in the afternoon. I could not sleep that night; its hours seemed interminably long, though it was one of the shortest of the year. The slow way in which we had come down had brought us to the long days and heats of June; and everybody knows what the climate of New Orleans is at that period of the year.

And now occurred one of those sudden, marked interpositions of Providence, by which in a moment, the whole current of a human being's life is changed; one of those slight and, at first, unappreciated contingencies, by which the faith that man's extremity is God's opportunity is kept alive. Little did I think, when just before daylight Master Amos called me and told me he felt sick, how much my future was bound up in those few words. His stomach was disordered, and I advised him to lie down again, thinking it would soon pass off. Before long he felt worse, and it was soon evident that the river-fever was upon him. He became rapidly ill, and by eight o'clock in the morning was utterly prostrate. The tables were now turned. I was no longer property, no longer a brute-beast to be bought and sold, but his only friend in the midst of strangers. Oh, how different was his tone from what it had been the day before! He was now the supplicant, a poor, terrified object, afraid of death, and writhing with pain; there lay the late arbiter of my destiny. How he besought me to forgive him! "Stick to me, Sie! Stick to me, Sie! Don't leave me, don't leave me. I'm sorry I was going to sell you." Sometimes he would say he had only been joking, and never intended to part with me. Yes, the tables were utterly turned. He entreated me to dispatch matters, sell the flat-boat in which we had been living, and get him and his trunk, containing the proceeds of the trip, on board the steamer as quickly as possible. I attended to all his requests, and by twelve o'clock that day, he was in one of the cabins of the steamer appropriated to sick passengers.

O my God! how my heart sang jubilees of praise to Thee, as the steamboat swung loose from the levee and breasted the mighty tide of the Mississippi! Away from this land of bondage and death! Away from misery and despair! Once more exulting hope possessed me, and I thought, if I do not now find my way to freedom, may God never give me a chance again!

Before we had proceeded many hours on our voyage, my young master appeared to be better. The change of air in a measure revived him; and well it was for him that such was the case. Short as his illness had been, the fever had raged like a fire, and he was already near death. I watched and nursed him like a mother; for all remembrance of personal wrong was obliterated at the sight of his peril. His eyes followed me in entreaty wherever I went. His strength was so entirely gone, that he could neither speak nor move a limb, and could only indicate his wish for a teaspoonful of gruel, or something to moisten his throat, by a feeble motion of his lips. I nursed him carefully and constantly. Nothing else could have saved his life. It hung by a thread for a long time. We were twelve days in reaching home, for the water was low at that season, particularly in the Ohio River; and when we arrived at our landing, he was still unable to speak, and could only be moved on a litter. Something of this sort was fixed up at the landing, on which he could be carried to the house, which was five miles off; and I got a party of the slaves belonging to the estate to form relays for the purpose. As we approached the house, the surprise at seeing me back again, and the perplexity to imagine what I was bringing along, with such a party, were extreme; but the discovery was soon made which explained the strange appearance; and the grief of father and mother, brothers and sisters, made itself seen and heard. Loud and long were the lamentations over poor Amos; and when the family came a little to themselves, great were the commendations bestowed upon me for my care of him and of the property.

Although we reached home by the 10th of July, it was not until the middle of August that Master Amos was well enough to leave his chamber. To do him justice, he manifested strong gratitude towards me. Almost his first words after recovering his strength sufficiently to talk, were in commendation of my conduct. "If I had sold him I should have died." On the rest of the family no permanent impression seemed to have been made. The first few words of praise were all I ever received. I was set at my old work. My merits, whatever they were, instead of exciting sympathy or any feeling of attachment to me, seemed only to enhance my market-value in their eyes. I saw that my master's only thought was to render me profitable to himself. From him I had nothing to hope, and I turned my thoughts to myself and my own energies.

Before long I felt assured another attempt would

be made to dispose of me. Providence seemed to have interfered once to defeat the scheme, but I could not expect such extraordinary circumstances to be repeated ; and I was bound to do everything in my power to secure myself and my family from the wicked conspiracy of Isaac and Amos Riley against my life, as well as against my natural rights, and those which I had acquired, even under the barbarous laws of slavery, by the money I had paid for myself. If Isaac had only been honest enough to adhere to his bargain, I would have adhered to mine, and paid him all I had promised. But his attempt to kidnap me again, after having pocketed three-fourths of my market value, in my opinion, absolved me from all obligation to pay him any more, or to continue in a position which exposed me to his machinations.

F

CHAPTER XII.

ESCAPE FROM BONDAGE.

SOLITARY MUSINGS.——PREPARATIONS FOR FLIGHT.——A LONG GOOD
NIGHT TO MASTER.——A DARK NIGHT ON THE RIVER.——NIGHT
JOURNEYS IN INDIANA.——ON THE BRINK OF STARVATION.——A
KIND WOMAN.——A NEW STYLE OF DRINKING CUP.——REACH
CINCINNATI.

DURING the bright and hopeful days I spent in
Ohio, while away on my preaching tour, I had
heard much of the course pursued by fugitives from
slavery, and became acquainted with a number of
benevolent men engaged in helping them on their
way. Canada was often spoken of as the only sure
refuge from pursuit, and that blessed land was now
the desire of my longing heart. Infinite toils and
perils lay between me and that haven of promise,
enough to daunt the stoutest heart; but the fire
behind me was too hot and fierce to let me pause to
consider them. I knew the North Star——blessed be
God for setting it in the heavens! Like the Star of
Bethlehem, it announced where my salvation lay.
Could I follow it through forest, and stream, and
field, it would guide my feet in the way of hope. I
thought of it as my God-given guide to the land of
promise far away beneath its light. I knew that it
had led thousands of my poor, hunted brethren to

freedom and blessedness. I felt energy enough in my own breast to contend with privation and danger; and had I been a free, untrammelled man, knowing no tie of father or husband, and concerned for my own safety only, I would have felt all difficulties light in view of the hope that was set before me. But, alas! I had a wife and four dear children; how should I provide for them? Abandon them I could not; no! not even for the blessed boon of freedom. They, too, must go. They, too, must share with me the life of liberty.

It was not without long thought upon the subject that I devised a plan of escape. But at last I matured it. My mind fully made up, I communicated the intention to my wife. She was overwhelmed with terror. With a woman's instinct she clung to hearth and home. She knew nothing of the wide world beyond, and her imagination peopled it with unseen horrors. She said, "We shall die in the wilderness, we shall be hunted down with bloodhounds; we shall be brought back and whipped to death." With tears and supplications she besought me to remain at home, contented. In vain I explained to her our liability to be torn asunder at any moment; the horrors of the slavery I had lately seen; the happiness we should enjoy together in a land of freedom, safe from all pursuing harm. She had not suffered the bitterness of my lot, nor felt the same longing for deliverance. She was a poor, timid, unreasoning slave-woman.

I argued the matter with her at various times, till I was satisfied that argument alone would not prevail. I then told her deliberately, that though it would be a cruel trial for me to part with her, I would nevertheless do it, and take all the children with me except the youngest, rather than remain at home, only to be forcibly torn from her, and sent down to linger out a wretched existence in the dens I had lately visited. Again she wept and entreated, but I was sternly resolute. The whole night long she fruitlessly urged me to relent; exhausted and maddened, I left her, in the morning, to go to my work for the day. Before I had gone far, I heard her voice calling me, and waiting till I came up, she said, at last, she would go with me. Blessed relief! my tears of joy flowed faster than had hers of grief.

Our cabin, at this time, was near the landing. The plantation itself extended the whole five miles from the house to the river. There were several distinct farms, all of which I was overseeing, and therefore I was riding about from one to another every day. Our oldest boy was at the house with Master Amos; the rest of the children were with my wife.

The chief practical difficulty that had weighed upon my mind, was connected with the youngest two of the children. They were of three and two years respectively, and of course would have to be carried. Both stout and healthy, they were a heavy burden, and my wife had declared that I should break down under it before I had got five miles from home. Sometime previously I had directed her to make me a large knapsack of tow-cloth, large enough to hold them both, and arranged with strong straps to go round my shoulders. This done, I had practised carrying them night after night, both to test my own strength and accustom them to submit to it. To them it was fine fun, and to my great joy I found I could manage them successfully. My wife's consent was given on Thursday morning, and I resolved to start on the night of the following Saturday. Sunday was a holiday; on Monday and Tuesday I was to be away on farms distant from the house; thus several days would elapse before I should be missed, and by that time I should have got a good start.

At length the eventful night arrived. All things were ready, with the single exception that I had not yet obtained my master's permission for little Tom to visit his mother. About sundown I went up to the great house to report my work, and after talking for a time, started off, as usual, for home; when, suddenly appearing to recollect something I had forgotten, I turned carelessly back, and said, " Oh, Master Amos, I most forgot. Tom's mother wants to know if you won't let him come down a few days; she wants to mend his clothes and fix him up a little." " Yes, boy, yes; he can go." " Thankee, Master Amos; good night, good night. The Lord bless you!" In spite of myself I threw a good deal of emphasis into my farewell. I could not refrain from an inward chuckle at the thought—how long a good night that will be! The coast was all clear now, and, as I trudged along home, I took an affectionate look at the well-known objects on my way. Strange to say, sorrow mingled with my joy; but no man can live long anywhere without feeling some attachment to the soil on which he labours.

It was about the middle of September, and by nine o'clock all was ready. It was a dark, moonless night, when we got into the little skiff, in which I had induced a fellow-slave to set us across the river. It was an anxious moment. We sat still as death. In the middle of the stream the good fellow said to me, " It will be the end of me if this is ever found out; but you won't be brought back alive, Sie, will you?" " Not if I can help it," I replied ; and I thought of the pistols and knife I had bought some time before of a poor white. "And if they're too many for you, and you get seized, you'll never tell my part in this business ? " " Not if I'm shot through like a sieve." " That's all," said he, " and God help you." Heaven reward him. He, too, has since followed in my steps; and many a time in a land of freedom have we talked over that dark night on the river.

In due time we landed on the Indiana shore. A hearty, grateful farewell was spoken, such as none but companions in danger can utter, and I heard the oars of the skiff propelling him home. There I stood in the darkness, my dear ones with me, and the dim unknown future before us. But there was little time for reflection. Before daylight should come on, we must put as many miles behind us as possible, and be safely hidden in the woods. We had no friends to look to for assistance, for the population in that section of the country was then bitterly hostile to the fugitive. If discovered, we should be seized and lodged in jail. In God was our only hope. Fervently did I pray to Him as we trudged on cautiously and stealthily, as fast as the darkness and the feebleness of my wife and boys would allow. To her, indeed, I was compelled to talk sternly ; she trembled like a leaf, and even then implored me to return.

For a fortnight we pressed steadily on, keeping to the road during the night, hiding whenever a chance vehicle or horseman was heard, and during the day burying ourselves in the woods. Our provisions were rapidly giving out. Two days before reaching Cincinnati they were utterly exhausted. All night long the children cried with hunger, and my poor wife loaded me with reproaches for bringing them into such misery. It was a bitter thing to hear them cry, and God knows I needed encouragement myself. My limbs were weary, and my back and shoulders raw with the burden I carried. A fearful dread of detection ever pursued me, and I would start out of my sleep in terror, my heart beating against my ribs, expecting to find the dogs and slave-hunters after me. Had I been alone, I would have borne starvation, even to exhaustion, before I would have ventured in sight of a house in quest of food. But now something must be done ; it was necessary to run the risk of exposure by daylight upon the road.

The only way to proceed was to adopt a bold course. Accordingly, I left our hiding-place, took to the road, and turned towards the south, to lull any suspicion that might be aroused were I to be seen going the other way. Before long I came to a house.   A furious dog rushed out at me, and his master following to quiet him, I asked if he would sell me a little bread and meat.   He was a surly fellow.   "No, I have nothing for niggers!"   At the next, I succeeded no better, at first.   The man of the house met me in the same style; but his wife, hearing our conversation, said to her husband, "How can you treat any human being so? If a dog was hungry I would give him something to eat." She then added, "We have children, and who knows but they may some day need the help of a friend." The man laughed and told her that if she took care of niggers, he wouldn't.   She asked me to come in, loaded a plate with venison and bread, and, when I laid it into my handkerchief, and put a quarter of a dollar on the table, she quietly took it up and put it in my handkerchief, with an additional quantity of venison.   I felt the hot tears roll down my cheeks as she said, "God bless you;" and I hurried away to bless my starving wife and little ones.

A little while after eating the venison, which was quite salt, the children became very thirsty, and groaned and sighed so that I went off stealthily, breaking the bushes to keep my path, to find water. I found a little rill, and drank a large draught. Then I tried to carry some in my hat; but, alas! it leaked.   Finally, I took off both shoes, which luckily had no holes in them, rinsed them out, filled them with water, and carried it to my family.   They drank it with great delight.   I have since then sat at splendidly-furnished tables in Canada, the United

States, and England; but never did I see any human beings relish anything more than my poor famishing little ones did that refreshing draught out of their father's shoes. That night we made a long run, and two days afterwards we reached Cincinnati.

CHAPTER XIII.

JOURNEY TO CANADA.

GOOD SAMARITANS.—ALONE IN THE WILDERNESS.—MEET SOME
INDIANS.—REACH SANDUSKY.—ANOTHER FRIEND.—ALL ABOARD.
—BUFFALO.—A "FREE NIGGER."—FRENZY OF JOY ON REACHING
CANADA.

I now felt comparatively at home. Before entering
the town I hid my wife and children in the
woods, and then walked on alone in search of my
friends. They welcomed me warmly, and just after
dusk my wife and children were brought in, and we
found ourselves hospitably cheered and refreshed.
Two weeks of exposure to incessant fatigue, anxiety,
rain, and chill, made it indescribably sweet to enjoy
once more the comfort of rest and shelter.

I have sometimes heard harsh and bitter words
spoken of those devoted men who were banded
together to succour and bid God speed to the hunted
fugitive; men who, through pity for the suffering,
voluntarily exposed themselves to hatred, fines, and
imprisonment. If there be a God who will have
mercy on the merciful, great will be their reward.
In the great day when men shall stand in judgment
before the Divine Master, crowds of the outcast and
forsaken of earth, will gather around them, and in
joyful tones bear witness, " We were hungry and ye

gave us meat, thirsty and ye gave us drink, naked
and ye clothed us, sick and ye visited us." And He
Who has declared that, "inasmuch as ye have done
it unto the least of these My brethren, ye have done
it unto Me," will accept the attestation, and hail
them with His welcome, "Come ye blessed of My
Father." Their glory shall yet be proclaimed from
the house-tops, and may that "peace of God which
the world can neither give nor take away" dwell
richly in their hearts!

Among such as those—good Samaritans, of whom
the Lord would say, "Go ye and do likewise,"—our
lot was now cast. Carefully they provided for our
welfare until our strength was recruited, and then
they set us thirty miles on our way by waggon.

We followed the same course as before—travelling
by night and resting by day—till we arrived at the
Scioto, where we had been told we should strike the
military road of General Hull, made in the last war
with Great Britain, and might then safely travel by
day. We found the road, accordingly, by the large
sycamore and elms which marked its beginning, and
entered upon it with fresh spirits early in the day.
Nobody had told us that it was cut through the
wilderness, and I had neglected to provide any food,
thinking we should soon come to some habitation,
where we could be supplied. But we travelled on
all day without seeing one, and lay down at night,
hungry and weary enough. The wolves were howling
around us, and though too cowardly to approach,
their noise terrified my poor wife and children.
Nothing remained to us in the morning but a little

piece of dried beef, too little, indeed, to satisfy our cravings, but enough to afflict us with intolerable thirst. I divided most of this amongst us, and then we started for a second day's tramp in the wilderness. A painful day it was to us. The road was rough, the underbrush tore our clothes and exhausted our strength; trees that had been blown down, blocked the way; we were faint with hunger, and no prospect of relief opened up before us. We spoke little, but steadily struggled along; I with my babes on my back, my wife aiding the two other children to climb over the fallen trunks and force themselves through the briers. Suddenly, as I was plodding along a little ahead of my wife and the boys, I heard them call me, and turning round saw my wife prostrate on the ground. "Mother's dying," cried Tom; and when I reached her, it seemed really so. From sheer exhaustion she had fallen in surmounting a log. Distracted with anxiety, I feared she was gone. For some minutes no sign of life was manifest; but after a time she opened her eyes, and finally recovering enough to take a few mouthfuls of the beef, her strength returned, and we once more went bravely on our way. I cheered the sad group with hopes I was far from sharing myself. For the first time I was nearly ready to abandon myself to despair. Starvation in the wilderness was the doom that stared me and mine in the face. But again, "man's extremity was God's opportunity."

We had not gone far, and I suppose it was about three o'clock in the afternoon, when we discerned some persons approaching us at no great distance.

We were instantly on the alert, as we could hardly expect them to be friends. The advance of a few paces showed me they were Indians, with packs on their shoulders; and they were so near that if they were hostile it would be useless to try to escape. So I walked along boldly, till we came close upon them. They were bent down with their burdens, and had not raised their eyes till now; and when they did so, and saw me coming towards them, they looked at me in a frightened sort of a way for a moment, and then, setting up a peculiar howl, turned round, and ran as fast as they could. There were three or four of them, and what they were afraid of I could not imagine. There was no doubt they were frightened, and we heard their wild and prolonged howl, as they ran, for a mile or more. My wife was alarmed, too, and thought they were merely running back to collect more of a party, and then would come and murder us; and she wanted to turn back. I told her they were numerous enough to do that, if they wanted to, without help; and that as for turning back, I had had quite too much of the road behind us, and that it would be a ridiculous thing that both parties should run away. If they were disposed to run, I would follow. We did follow, and the noise soon ceased. As we advanced, we could discover Indians peeping at us from behind the trees, and dodging out of sight if they thought we were looking at them. Presently we came upon their wigwams, and saw a fine-looking, stately Indian, with his arms folded, waiting for us to approach. He was, apparently, the chief; and, saluting us civilly, he soon discovered we were human beings, and spoke to his young men, who were scattered about, and made them come in and give up their foolish fears. And now curiosity seemed to prevail. Each one wanted to touch the children, who were as shy as partridges with their long life in the woods ; and as they shrunk away, and uttered a little cry of alarm, the Indian would jump back too, as if he thought they would bite him. However, a little while sufficed to make them understand whither we were going, and what we needed; and then they supplied our wants, fed us bountifully, and gave us a comfortable wigwam for our night's rest. The next day we resumed our march, having ascertained from the Indians that we were only about twenty-five miles from the lake. They sent some of their young men to point out the place where we were to turn off, and parted from us with as much kindness as possible.

In passing over the part of Ohio near the lake, where such an extensive, plain is found, we came to a spot overflowed by a stream, across which the road passed. I forded it first, with the help of a sounding-pole, and then taking the children on my back, first the two little ones, and then the others, one at a time, and, lastly, my wife, I succeeded in getting them safely across. At this time the skin was worn from my back to an extent almost equal to the size of the knapsack.

One night more was passed in the woods, and in the course of the next forenoon, we came out upon the wide, treeless plain which lies south and west of Sandusky city. The houses of the village were in

plain sight. About a mile from the lake I hid my
wife and children in the bushes, and pushed forward.
I was attracted by a house on the left, between
which and a small coasting vessel, a number of men
were passing and repassing with great activity.
Promptly deciding to approach them, I drew near,
and scarcely had I come within hailing distance,
when the captain of the schooner cried out, " Hollo
there, man ! you want to work ? " " Yes, sir ! "
shouted I. " Come along, come along ; I'll give
you a shilling an hour. Must get off with this
wind." As I came near, he said, " Oh, you can't
work ; you're crippled." " Can't I ? " said I ; and
in a minute I had hold of a bag of corn, and followed the gang in emptying it into the hold. I
took my place in the line of labourers next to a
coloured man, and soon got into conversation with
him. " How far is it to Canada ? " He gave me a
peculiar look, and in a minute I saw he knew all.
" Want to go to Canada ? Come along with us,
then. Our captain's a fine fellow. We're going to
Buffalo." " Buffalo ; how far is that from Canada ? "
" Don't you know, man ? Just across the river."
I now opened my mind frankly to him, and told
him about my wife and children. " I'll speak to the
captain," said he. He did so, and in a moment the
captain took me aside, and said, " The Doctor says
you want to go to Buffalo with your family." " Yes,
sir." " Well, why not go with me ! " was his frank
reply. " Doctor says you've got a family." " Yes,
sir." " Where do you stop ? " " About a mile
back." " How long have you been here ? " " No

time,", I answered, after a moment's hesitation.
"Come, my good fellow, tell us all about it. You're
running away, ain't you?" I saw he was a friend,
and opened my heart to him. "How long will it
take you to get ready?" "Be here in half an hour,
sir." "Well, go along and get them." Off I
started; but, before I had run fifty feet, he called
me back. "Stop," said he; "you go on getting
the grain in. When we get off, I'll lay to over
opposite that island, and send a boat back. There's a
lot of regular nigger-catchers in the town below, and
they might suspect if you brought your party out of
the bush by daylight." I worked away with a will.
Soon the two or three hundred bushels of corn were
aboard, the hatches fastened down, the anchor raised,
and the sails hoisted.

I watched the vessel with intense interest as she
left her moorings. Away she went before the free
breeze. Already she seemed beyond the spot at
which the captain agreed to lay to, and still she
flew along. My heart sank within me; so near deliverance, and again to have my hopes blasted, again
to be cast on my own resources! I felt that they
had been making sport of my misery. The sun
had sunk to rest, and the purple and gold of the
west were fading away into grey. Suddenly, however, as I gazed with a weary heart, the vessel swung
round into the wind, the sails flapped, and she stood
motionless. A moment more, and a boat was lowered
from her stern, and with a steady stroke made for
the point at which I stood. I felt that my hour of

release had come.   On she came, and in ten minutes she rode up handsomely on to the beach.

My black friend and two sailors jumped out, and we started off at once for my wife and children.   To my horror, they were gone from the place where I left them.   Overpowered with fear, I supposed they had been found and carried off.   There was no time to lose, and the men told me I would have to go alone. Just at the point of despair, however, I stumbled on one of the children.   My wife, it seemed, alarmed at my long absence, had given up all for lost, and supposed I had fallen into the hands of the enemy. When she heard my voice, mingled with those of the others, she thought my captors were leading me back to make me discover my family, and in the extremity of her terror she had tried to hide herself. I had hard work to satisfy her.   Our long habits of concealment and anxiety had rendered her suspicious of every one ; and her agitation was so great that for a time she was incapable of understanding what I said, and went on in a sort of paroxysm of distress and fear.   This, however, was soon over, and the kindness of my companions did much to facilitate the matter.

And now we were off for the boat.   It required little time to embark our baggage—one convenience, at least, of having nothing.   The men bent their backs with a will, and headed steadily for a light hung from the vessel's mast.   I was praising God in my soul.   Three hearty cheers welcomed us as we reached the schooner, and never till my dying day shall I forget the shout of the captain—he was a

G

Scotchman——"Coom up on deck, and clop your wings and craw like a rooster; you're a free nigger as sure as you're a live mon." Round went the vessel, the wind plunged into her sails as though innoculated with the common feeling—the water seethed and hissed past her sides. Man and nature, and, more than all, I felt the God of man and nature, who breathes love into the heart and maketh the winds His ministers, were with us. My happiness that night rose at times to positive pain. Unnerved by so sudden a change from destitution and danger to such kindness and blessed security, I wept like a child.

The next evening we reached Buffalo, but it was too late to cross the river that night. "You see those trees," said the noble-hearted captain, next morning, pointing to a group in the distance; "they grow on free soil, and as soon as your feet touch that, you're a *mon*. I want to see you go and be a freeman. I'm poor myself, and have nothing to give you; I only sail the boat for wages; but I'll see you across. Here, Green," said he to a ferryman, "what will you take this man and his family over for—he's got no money?" "Three shillings." He then took a dollar out of his pocket and gave it to me. Never shall I forget the spirit in which he spoke. He put his hand on my head and said, "Be a good fellow, won't you?" I felt streams of emotion running down in electric courses from head to foot. "Yes," said I; "I'll use my freedom well; I'll give my soul to God." He stood waving his hat as we pushed off for the opposite shore. God bless him! God bless him eternally! Amen!

It was the 28th of October, 1830, in the morning, when my feet first touched the Canada shore. I threw myself on the ground, rolled in the sand, seized handfuls of it and kissed them, and danced around, till, in the eyes of several who were present, I passed for a madman. "He's some crazy fellow," said a Colonel Warren, who happened to be there. "Oh no, master! don't you know? I'm free!" He burst into a shout of laughter. "Well, I never knew freedom make a man roll in the sand in such a fashion." Still I could not control myself. I hugged and kissed my wife and children, and, until the first exuberant burst of feeling was over, went on as before.

CHAPTER XIV.

NEW SCENES AND A NEW HOME.

A POOR MAN IN A STRANGE LAND.——BEGIN TO ACQUIRE PROPERTY.
——RESUME PREACHING.——BOYS GO TO SCHOOL.——WHAT GAVE ME A
DESIRE TO LEARN TO READ.——A DAY OF PRAYER IN THE WOODS.

THERE was not much time to be lost, though, in frolic even, at this extraordinary moment. I was a stranger in a strange land, and had to look about me at once for refuge and resource. I found a lodging for the night, and the next morning set about exploring the interior for the means of support. I knew nothing about the country or the people, but kept my eyes and ears open, and made such inquiries as opportunity afforded. I heard, in the course of the day, of a Mr. Hibbard, who lived some six or seven miles off. He was a rich man, as riches were counted there, had a large farm, and several small tenements on it, which he was in the habit of letting to his labourers. To him I went immediately, though the character given him by his neighbours was not, by any means, unexceptionably good. But I thought he was not, probably, any worse than those I had been accustomed to serve, and that I could get along with him, if honest and faithful work would satisfy him. In the afternoon I found him, and soon struck a bargain with him for employment. I asked him if there was any house where he would let me live. He said, "Yes," and led the way to an old two-story sort of shanty, into the lower story of which the pigs had broken, and had apparently made it their resting-place for some time. Still, it was a house, and I forthwith expelled the pigs, and set about cleaning it for the occupancy of a better sort of tenants. With the aid of hoe and shovel, hot water and a mop, I got the floor into a tolerable condition by midnight, and only then did I rest from my labour. The next day I brought the rest of the Hensons, the only furniture I had, to *my house*, and though there was nothing there but bare walls and floors, we were all in a state of great delight, and my wife laughed and acknowledged that it was better than a log cabin with an earth-floor. I begged some straw of Mr. Hibbard, and confining it by logs in the corners of the room, I made beds of it three feet thick, upon which we reposed luxuriously after our long fatigues.

Another trial awaited me which I had not anticipated. In consequence of the great exposures we had been through, my wife and all the children fell sick; and it was not without extreme peril that they escaped with their lives.

My employer soon found that my labour was of more value to him than that of those he was accustomed to hire; and as I consequently gained his favour, and his wife took quite a fancy to mine, we soon procured some of the comforts of life, while the necessaries of life, food and fuel, were abundant. I remained with Mr. Hibbard three years, sometimes working on shares, and sometimes for wages; and I managed in that time to procure some pigs, a cow, and a horse. Thus my condition gradually improved, and I felt that my toils and sacrifices for freedom had not been in vain. Nor were my labours for the improvement of myself and others, in more important things than food and clothing, without effect. It so happened that one of my Maryland friends arrived in this neighbourhood, and hearing of my being here, inquired if I ever preached now, and spread the reputation I had acquired elsewhere for my gifts in the pulpit. I had said nothing myself, and had not intended to say anything of my having ever officiated in that way. I went to meeting with others, when I had an opportunity, and enjoyed the quiet of the Sabbath when there was no assembly. I could not refuse to labour in this field, however, when afterwards desired to do so; and I was from this time frequently called upon, not by blacks alone, but by all classes in my vicinity—the comparatively educated, as well as the lamentably ignorant—to speak to them on their duty, responsibility, and immortality, on their obligations to themselves, their Saviour, and their Maker.

I am aware it must seem strange to many that a man so ignorant, unable to read, and having heard so little as I had of religion, natural or revealed, should be able to preach acceptably to persons who had enjoyed greater advantages than myself. I can explain it only by reference to our Saviour's comparison of the kingdom of heaven to a plant which may spring from a seed no bigger than a mustard-seed, and may yet reach such a size, that the birds of the air may take shelter therein. Religion is not so much knowledge as wisdom; and observation upon what passes without, and reflection upon what passes within a man's heart, will give him a larger growth in grace than is imagined by the devoted adherents of creeds, or the confident followers of Christ, who call Him "Lord, Lord," but do not the things which He says.

Mr. Hibbard was good enough to give my eldest boy, Tom, two quarters' schooling, to which the schoolmaster added more, of his own kindness, so that my boy learned to read fluently and well. It was a great advantage, not only to him, but to me; for I used to get him to read much to me in the Bible, especially on Sunday mornings, when I was going to preach; and I could easily commit to memory a few verses, or a chapter, from hearing him read it over.

One beautiful summer Sabbath I rose early, and called him to come and read to me. "Where shall I read, father?" "Anywhere, my son," I answered, for I knew not how to direct him. He opened upon Psalm ciii., "Bless the Lord, O my soul: and all that is within me, bless His holy name;" and as he read this beautiful outpouring of gratitude, which I now first heard, my heart melted within me. I recalled, with all the rapidity of which thought is capable, the whole current of my life; and, as I remembered the dangers and afflictions from which the Lord had delivered me, and compared my present condition with what it had been, not only my heart but my eyes overflowed, and I could neither check nor conceal the emotion which overpowered me.   The words, "Bless the Lord, O my soul," with which the Psalm begins and ends, were all I needed, or could use, to express the fulness of my thankful heart.   When he had finished, Tom turned to me and asked, "Father, who was David?"   He had observed my excitement, and added, "He writes pretty, don't he?" and then repeated his question. It was a question I was utterly unable to answer.   I had never heard of David, but could not bear to acknowledge my ignorance to my own child.   So I answered, evasively, "He was a man of God, my son."   "I suppose so," said he, "but I want to know something more about him.   Where did he live?   What did he do?"   As he went on questioning me, I saw it was in vain to attempt to escape, and so I told him frankly I did not know.   "Why, father," said he, "can't you read?"   This was a worse question than the other, and, if I had any pride in me at the moment, it took it all out of me pretty quick.   It was a direct question, and must have a direct answer; so I told him at once I could not.   "Why not?" said he.   "Because I never had an opportunity to learn, nor anybody to teach me." "Well, you can learn now, father."   "No, my son, I am too old, and have not time enough.   I must work all day, or you would not have enough to eat." "Then you might do it at night."   "But still there is nobody to teach me.   I can't afford to pay anybody for it, and, of course, no one can do it for nothing." "Why, father, *I'll teach you.*   I can do it, I know.

And then you'll know so much more that you will be able to talk better, and preach better." The little fellow was so earnest, there was no resisting him ; but it is hard to describe the conflicting feelings within me at such a proposition from such a quarter. I was delighted with the conviction that my children would have advantages I had never enjoyed ; but it was no slight mortification to think of being instructed by my young son. Yet ambition, and a true desire to learn, for the good it would do my own mind, conquered the shame, and I agreed to try. But I did not reach this state of mind instantly.

I was greatly moved by the conversation I had with Tom, so much so, that I could not undertake to preach that day. The congregation were disappointed, and I passed the Sunday in solitary reflection in the woods. I was too much engrossed with the multitude of my thoughts to return home to dinner, and spent the whole day in secret meditation and prayer, trying to compose myself, and ascertain my true position. It was not difficult to see that my predicament was one of profound ignorance, and that I ought to use every opportunity of enlightening it. I began to take lessons of Tom, therefore, immediately, and followed it up every evening, by the light of a pine knot, or some hickory bark, which was the only light I could afford. Weeks passed, and my progress was so slow that poor Tom was almost discouraged, and used to drop asleep sometimes, and whine a little over my dulness, and talk to me very much as a schoolmaster talks to a stupid boy, till I began to be afraid that my age, nearly fifty, my want of practice in looking at such little scratches, the daily fatigue, and the dim light, would be effectual preventives of my ever acquiring the art of reading. But Tom's perseverance and mine conquered at last, and in the course of the winter I did really learn to read a little.

It was, and has been ever since, a great comfort to me to have made this acquisition ; though it has made me comprehend better the terrible abyss of ignorance into which I had been plunged all my previous life. It made me also feel more deeply and bitterly the oppression under which I had toiled and groaned, the crushing and cruel nature of which I had not appreciated, till I found out, in some slight degree, from what I had been debarred. At the same time it made me more anxious than before, to do something for the rescue and the elevation of those who were suffering the same evils I had endured, and who did not know how degraded and ignorant they really were.

CHAPTER XV.

LIFE IN CANADA.

AFTER about three years had passed, I improved my condition again by taking service with a gentleman by the name of Riseley, whose residence was only a few miles distant. He was a man of more elevation of mind than Mr. Hibbard, and of superior abilities. At his place I began to reflect, more and more, upon the circumstances of the blacks, who were already somewhat numerous in this region. I was not the only one who had escaped from the States, and had settled on the first spot in Canada which they had reached. Several hundreds of coloured persons were in the neighbourhood, and, in the first joy of their deliverance, they were living in a way, which, I could see, led to little or no progress in improvement. They were content to have the proceeds of their labour at their own command, and had not the ambition for, or the perception of what was within their easy reach, if they did but know it. They were generally working for hire upon the lands of others, and had not yet dreamed of becoming independent proprietors themselves. It soon became my great object to awaken

them to a sense of the advantages which were
within their grasp; and Mr. Riseley, seeing clearly
the justness of my views, and willing to co-operate
with me in the attempt to make them generally
known among the blacks, permitted me to call
meetings at his house of those who were known to
be amongst the most intelligent and successful of our
class. At these meetings we considered and discussed the subject, till we were all of one mind; and
it was agreed, among the ten or twelve of us who
assembled at them, that we would invest our earnings
in land, and undertake the task—which, though no
light one certainly, would yet soon reward us for our
effort—of settling upon wild lands, which we could
call our own, and where every tree which we felled,
and every bushel of corn we raised, would be for
ourselves; in other words, where we could secure all
the profits of our own labour.

The advantages of such a course of procedure
have been exemplified for two hundred years and
more, by the people who have thereby acquired an
indestructible character for energy, enterprise, and
self-reliance. It was precisely this energetic spirit
which I wished to instil into my fellow-slaves, if
possible; and I was not deterred from the task by
the perception of the immense contrast in all their
habits and character generated by long ages of freedom and servitude, activity and sloth, independence
and subjection. My associates agreed with me, and
we resolved to select some spot among the many
offered to our choice, where we could colonize, and
raise our own crops, eat our own bread, and be, in

short, our own masters. I was deputed to explore
the country, and find a place to which I would be
willing to migrate myself; and they all said they
would go with me, whenever such a one should be
found. I set out accordingly in the autumn of 1834,
and travelled on foot all over the extensive region
between lakes Ontario, Erie, and Huron. When I
came to the territory east of Lake St. Clair and
Detroit River, I was strongly impressed with its
fertility and its superiority, for all our purposes, to
any other spot I had seen. I determined this should
be the place; and so reported, on my return, to my
future companions. They were wisely cautious,
however, and sent me off again in the summer, that
I might see it at the opposite seasons of the year,
and be better able to judge of its advantages. I
found no reason to change my opinion, but upon
going farther towards the head of Lake Erie, I
discovered an extensive tract of government-land,
which, for some years, had been granted to a Mr.
McCormick upon certain conditions, and which he
had rented out to settlers upon such terms as he
could obtain. This land being already cleared,
offered some advantages for the immediate raising
of crops, which were not to be overlooked by persons whose resources were so limited as ours. We
determined to go there first, for a time, and with
the proceeds of what we could earn there, to make
our purchases in Dawn afterwards. This plan was
followed, and some dozen or more of us settled upon
those lands the following spring, and accumulated
something by the crops of wheat and tobacco we
were able to raise.

I discovered, before long, that McCormick had not complied with the conditions of his grant, and was not, therefore, entitled to the rent he exacted from the settlers. I was advised by Sir John Cockburn, to whom I applied on the subject, to appeal to the legislature for relief. We did so ; and though McCormick was able, by the aid of his friends, to defeat us for one year, yet we succeeded the next, upon a second appeal, and were freed from all rent thereafter, so long as we remained. Still, this was not our own land. The government, though it demanded no rent, might set up the land for sale at any time, and then we should, probably, be driven off by wealthier purchasers, with the entire loss of all our improvements, and with no retreat provided. It was manifest that it was altogether better for us to purchase before competition was invited; and we kept this fully in mind during the time we stayed there. We remained in this position six or seven years ; and all this while the coloured population was increasing rapidly around us, and spreading very fast into the interior settlements and the large towns. The immigration from the United States was incessant, and some, I am willing to admit, were brought hither with my knowledge and connivance ; and I will now proceed to give a short account of the plans and operations I had arranged for the liberation of some of my brethren, which I hope may prove interesting to the reader.

CHAPTER XVI.

CONDUCTING SLAVES TO CANADA.

THE degraded and hopeless condition of a slave can never be properly felt by him while he remains in such a position. After I had tasted the blessings of freedom, my mind reverted to those whom I knew were groaning in captivity, and I at once proceeded to take measures to free as many as I could. I thought that, by using exertion, numbers might make their escape as I did, if they had some practical advice how to proceed.

I was once attending a very large meeting at Fort Erie, at which a great many coloured people were present. In the course of my preaching, I tried to impress upon them the importance of the obligations they were under ; first, to God, for their deliverance ; and then, secondly, to their fellow-men, to do all that was in their power to bring others out of bondage. In the congregation was a man named James Lightfoot, who was of a very active temperament, and had obtained his freedom by fleeing to Canada, but had never thought of his family and friends whom he had left behind, until the time he heard me speaking, although he himself had been free for some five years. However, that day the cause was brought home to his heart. When the service was concluded, he begged to have an interview with me, to which I gladly acceded, and an arrangement was made for further conversation on the same subject one week from that time. He then informed me where he came from, also to whom he belonged, and that he had left behind a dear father and mother, three sisters and four brothers; and that they lived on the Ohio River, not far from the city of Maysville. He said that he never saw his duty towards them to be so clear and unmistakable as he did at that time, and professed himself ready to co-operate in any measures that might be devised for their release. During the short period of his freedom he had accumulated some little property, the whole of which, he stated, he would cheerfully devote to carrying out those measures; for he had no rest, night nor day, since the meeting above mentioned.

I was not able at that time to propose what was best to be done, and thus we parted; but in a few days he came to see me again on the same errand. Seeing the agony of his heart in behalf of his kindred, I consented to commence the painful and dangerous task of endeavouring to free those whom he so much loved. I left my own family in the hands of no other save God, and commenced the journey alone, on foot, and travelled thus about four hundred miles. But the Lord furnished me with strength sufficient for the undertaking. I passed through the States of New York, Pennsylvania, and Ohio—free States, so called—crossed the Ohio River into Kentucky, and ultimately found his friends in the place he had described.

I was an entire stranger to them, but I took with me a small token of their brother who was gone, which they at once recognised; and this was to let them know that he had gone to Canada, the land of freedom, and had now sent a friend to assist them in making their escape. This created no little excitement. But his parents had become so far advanced in years that they could not undertake the fatigue; his sisters had a number of children, and they could not travel; his four brothers and a nephew were young men, and sufficiently able for the journey, but the thought of leaving their father, and mother, and sisters, was too painful; and they also considered it unsafe to make the attempt then, for fear that the excitement and grief of their friends might betray them; so they declined going at that time, but promised that they would go in a year if I would return for them.

To this I assented, and then went between forty and fifty miles into the interior of Kentucky, having heard that there was a large party ready to attempt their escape if they had a leader to direct their movements. I travelled by night, resting by day, and at length reached Bourbon county, the place where I expected to find these people. After a delay of about a week, spent in discussing plans, making arrangements, and other matters, I found that there were about thirty collected from different States, who

H

were disposed to make the attempt.   At length, on a Saturday night, we started.   The agony of parting can be better conceived than described ; as, in their case, husbands were leaving their wives, mothers their children, and children their parents.   This, at first sight, will appear strange, and even incredible ; but, when we take into consideration the fact, that at any time they were liable to be separated, by being sold to what are termed "nigger traders," and the probability that such an event would take place, it will, I think, cease to excite any surprise.

We succeeded in crossing the Ohio River in safety, and arrived in Cincinnati the third night after our departure.   Here we procured assistance ; and, after stopping a short time to rest, we started for Richmond, Indiana.   This is a town which had been settled by Quakers, and there we found friends indeed, who at once helped us on our way, without loss of time ; and after a difficult journey of two weeks, through the wilderness, we reached Toledo, Ohio, a town on the south-western shore of Lake Erie, and there we took passage for Canada, which we reached in safety.   I then went home to my family, taking with me a part of this large party, the rest finding their friends scattered in other towns, perfectly satisfied with my conduct in the matter, in being permitted to be the instrument of freeing such a number of my fellow-creatures.

CHAPTER XVII.

SECOND JOURNEY ON THE UNDERGROUND RAILROAD.

A SHOWER OF STARS.—KENTUCKIANS.—A STRATAGEM.—A PROVIDENCE.—CONDUCTED ACROSS THE MIAMI RIVER BY A COW.—ARRIVAL AT CINCINNATI.—ONE OF THE PARTY TAKEN ILL.—WE LEAVE HIM TO DIE.—MEET A "FRIEND."—A POOR WHITE MAN.—A STRANGE IMPRESSION.—ONCE MORE IN CANADA.

I REMAINED at home, working on my farm, until the next autumn, about the time I had promised to assist in the restoring to liberty the friends of James Lightfoot, the individual who had excited my sympathy at the meeting at Fort Erie. In pursuance of this promise, I again started on my long journey into Kentucky.

On my way, that strange occurrence happened, called the great meteoric shower. The heavens seemed broken up into streaks of light and falling stars. I reached Lancaster, Ohio, at three o'clock in the morning, found the village aroused, the bells ringing, and the people exclaiming, "The day of judgment is come!" I thought it was probably so; but felt that I was in the right business, and walked on through the village, leaving the terrified people behind. The stars continued to fall till the light of the sun appeared.

On arriving at Portsmouth, in the State of Ohio,

I had a very narrow escape from being detected. The place was frequented by a number of Kentuckians, who were quite ready to suspect a coloured man, if they saw anything unusual about him. I reached Portsmouth in the morning, and waited until two in the afternoon for the steamboat, so that I might not arrive in Maysville till after dark. While in the town I was obliged to resort to a stratagem, in order to avoid being questioned by the Kentuckians I saw in the place. To this end I procured some dried leaves, put them into a cloth and bound it all round my face, reaching nearly to my eyes, and pretended to be so seriously affected in my head and teeth as not to be able to speak. I then hung around the village till the time for the evening boat, so as to arrive at Maysville in the night. I was accosted by several during my short stay in Portsmouth, who appeared very anxious to get some particulars from me as to who I was, where I was going, and to whom I belonged. To all their numerous inquiries I merely shook my head, mumbled out indistinct answers, and acted so that they could not get anything out of me; and, by this artifice, I succeeded in avoiding any unpleasant consequences. I got on board the boat and reached Maysville, Kentucky, in the evening, about a fortnight from the time I had left Canada.

On landing, a wonderful providence happened to me. The second person I met in the street was Jefferson Lightfoot, brother of the James Lightfoot previously mentioned, and one of the party who had promised to escape if I would assist them. He stated that they were still determined to make the attempt, decided to put it into execution the following Saturday night, and preparations for the journey were at once commenced. The reason why Saturday night was chosen on this and the previous occasion was, that from not having to labour the next day, and being allowed to visit their families, they would not be missed until the time came for their usual appearance in the field, at which period they would be some eighty or a hundred miles away. During the interval I had to keep myself concealed by day, and used to meet them by night to make the necessary arrangements.

From fear of being detected, they started of without bidding their father or mother farewell, and then, in order to prevent the bloodhounds from following on our trail, we seized a skiff, a little below the city, and made our way down the river. It was not the shortest way, but it was the surest.

It was sixty-five miles from Maysville to Cincinnati, and we thought we could reach that city before daylight, and then take the stage for Sandusky. Our boat sprung a leak before we had got half way, and we narrowly escaped being drowned; providentially, however, we got to the shore before the boat sunk. We then took another boat, but this detention prevented us from arriving at Cincinnati in time for the stage. Day broke upon us when we were about ten miles above the city, and we were compelled to leave our boat from fear of being apprehended. This was an anxious time. However, we had got so far away that we knew there was no danger of being discovered by the hounds, and we thought we would go on foot. When we got within seven miles of Cincinnati, we came to the Miami River, and we could not reach the city without crossing it.

This was a great barrier to us, for the water appeared to be deep, and we were afraid to ask the loan of a boat, being apprehensive it might lead to our detection. We went first up and then down the river, trying to find a convenient crossing-place, but failed. I then said to my company, "Boys, let us go up the river and try again." We started, and after going about a mile we saw a cow coming out of a wood, and going to the river as though she intended to drink. Then said I, "Boys, let us go and see what the cow is about, it may be that she will tell us some news." I said this in order to cheer them up. One of them replied, in rather a peevish way, "Oh, that cow can't talk;" but I again urged them to come on. The cow remained until we approached her within a rod or two; she then walked into the river, and went straight across without swimming, which caused me to remark, "The Lord sent that cow to show us where to cross the river!" This has always seemed to me to be a very wonderful event.

Having urged our way with considerable haste, we were literally saturated with perspiration, though it was snowing at the time, and my companions thought that it would be highly dangerous for us to proceed through the water, especially as there was a large quantity of ice in the river. But as it was a ques-

JOURNEY ON THE UNDERGROUND RAILROAD. 115

tion of life or death with us, there was no time left for reasoning; I therefore advanced—they reluctantly following. The youngest of the Lightfoots, ere we reached halfway over the river, was seized with violent contraction of the limbs, which prevented further self-exertion on his part; he was, therefore, carried the remainder of the distance. After resorting to continued friction, he partially recovered, and we proceeded on our journey.

We reached Cincinnati about eleven on Sunday morning, too late for the stage that day; but having found some friends, we hid ourselves until Monday evening, when we recommenced our long and toilsome journey, through mud, rain, and snow, towards Canada. We had increased our distance about one hundred miles, by going out of our road to get among the Quakers. During our passage through the woods, the boy before referred to was taken alarmingly ill, and we were compelled to proceed with him on our backs; but finding this mode of conveying him exceedingly irksome, we constructed a kind of litter with our shirts and handkerchiefs laid across poles. By this time we got into the State of Indiana, so that we could travel by day as long as we kept to the woods. Our patient continued to get worse, and it appeared, both to himself and to us, that death would soon release him from his sufferings. He therefore begged to be left in some secluded spot, to die alone, as he feared that the delay occasioned by his having to be carried through the bush, might lead to the capture of the whole company. With very considerable reluctance we acceded to his request, and laid him in a sheltered place, with a full expectation that death would soon put an end to his sufferings. The poor fellow expressed his readiness to meet the last struggle in hope of eternal life. Sad, indeed, was the parting; and it was with difficulty we tore ourselves away.

We had not, however, proceeded more than two miles on our journey, when one of the brothers of the dying man made a sudden stop, and expressed his inability to proceed whilst he had the consciousness that he had left his brother to perish, in all probability, a prey to the devouring wolves. His grief was so great that we determined to return, and at length reached the spot, where we found the poor fellow apparently dying, moaning out with every breath a prayer to heaven. Words cannot describe the joyousness experienced by the Lightfoots when they saw their poor afflicted brother once more; they literally danced for joy. We at once prepared to resume our journey as we best could, and once more penetrated the bush. After making some progress, we saw, at a little distance on the road, a waggon approaching, and I immediately determined to ascertain whether some assistance could not be obtained.

I at length circumvented the road, so as to make it appear that I had been journeying in an opposite direction to that which the waggon was taking. When I came up with the driver, I bade him good day. He said, "Where is thee going?" "To Canada." I saw his coat, heard his *thee* and *thou*, and set him down for a Quaker. I therefore plainly told him our circumstances. He at once stopped his horses, and expressed his willingness to assist us. I returned to the place where my companions were in waiting for me, and soon had them in the presence of the Quaker. Immediately on viewing the sufferer he was moved to tears, and without delay turned his horses' heads, to proceed in the direction of his home, although he had intended to go to a distant market with a load of produce for sale. The reception we met with from the Quaker's family overjoyed our hearts, and the transports with which the poor men looked upon their brother, now so favourably circumstanced, cannot be described.

We remained with this happy family for the night, and received from them every kindness. It was arranged that the boy should remain behind, until, through the blessing of God, he should recover. We were kindly provided by them with a sack of biscuit and a joint of meat, and once more set our faces in the direction of Lake Erie.

After proceeding some distance on our road, we perceived a white man approaching, but as he was travelling alone, and on foot, we were not alarmed at his presence. It turned out that he had been residing for some time in the South, and although a free white man, his employers had attempted to castigate him; in return for which he had used violence, which made it necessary that he should at once escape. We travelled in company, and found that his presence was of signal service to us in delivering us out of the hands of the slave-hunters who were now on our track, and eagerly grasping after their prey. We had resolved on reaching the lake, a distance of forty miles, by the following morning; we, therefore, walked all night.

Just as the day was breaking, we reached a wayside tavern, immediately contiguous to the lake, and our white companion having knocked up the landland, ordered breakfast for six. Whilst our breakfast was in course of preparation, we dosed off into slumber, wearied with our long-continued exertion.

Just as our breakfast was ready, whilst half-asleep and half-awake, an impression came forcibly upon me that danger was nigh, and that I must at once leave the house. I immediately urged my companions to follow me out, which they were exceedingly unwilling to do; but as they had promised me submission, they at length yielded to my request. We retired to the yard at the side of the house, and commenced washing ourselves with the snow, which was now up to our knees. Presently we heard the tramping of horses, and were at once warned of the necessity of secreting ourselves. We crept beneath a pile of bushes, close at hand, which permitted a full view of the road. The horsemen came to a dead stop at the door of the house, and commenced their inquiries; my companions at once recognised the parties on horseback, and whispered their names to me. This was a critical moment, and the loud beatings of their hearts testified the dreadful alarm with which they viewed the scene. Had we been within doors, we should have been inevitably sacrificed. Our white friend proceeded to the door in advance of the landlord, and maintained his position. He was at once interrogated by the slave-hunters whether he had seen any negroes pass that way. He said, yes, he thought he had. Their number was demanded, and they were told about six, and that they were proceeding in the direction of Detroit; and that they might be some few miles on the road. They at once reigned their horses, which were greatly fatigued, through having been ridden all night, and were soon out of sight. We at length ventured into the house, and devoured breakfast in an incredibly short space of time. After what had transpired, the landlord became acquainted with our circumstances, and at once offered to sail us in his boat across to Canada. We were happy enough to have such an offer, and soon the white sail of our little bark was laying to the wind, and we were gliding along on our way, with the land of liberty in full view. Words cannot describe the feelings experienced by my companions as they neared the shore—their bosoms were swelling with inexpressible joy as they mounted the seats of the boat, ready, eagerly, to spring forward, that they might touch the soil of the freeman. And when they reached the shore, they danced and wept for joy, and kissed the earth on which they first stepped, no longer the SLAVE—but the FREE.

After the lapse of a few months, on one joyous Sabbath morning, I had the happiness of clasping the poor boy we had left in the kind care of the Quaker, no longer attenuated in frame, but robust and healthy, and surrounded by his family. Thus my joy was consummated, and superadded were the blessings of those who were ready to perish, which came upon me. It is one of the greatest sources of my happiness to know, that by similar means to those above narrated, I have been instrumental in delivering one hundred and eighteen human beings out of the cruel and merciless grasp of the slave-holder.

Mr. Frank Taylor, the owner of the Lightfoots, whose escape I have just narrated, soon after he missed his slaves, fell ill, and became quite deranged; on recovering, he was persuaded by his friends to free the remainder of the family of the Lightfoots, which he at length did, and after a short lapse of time, they all met each other in Canada, where they are now living.

CHAPTER XVIII.

HOME AT DAWN.

CONDITION IN CANADA.—EFFORTS IN BEHALF OF MY PEOPLE.—
REV. MR. WILSON.—A CONVENTION OF BLACKS.—MANUAL-LABOUR
SCHOOL.

I DID not find that our prosperity increased with
our numbers. The mere delight the slaves
took in their freedom, rendered them, at first, contented with a lot far inferior to that to which they
might have attained. Their ignorance often led
them to make unprofitable bargains, and they would
often hire wild land on short terms, and bind themselves to clear a certain number of acres. But by
the time they were cleared and fitted for cultivation,
and the lease was out, the landlords would take possession of the cleared land and raise a splendid crop on
it. The tenants would, very likely, start again on
just such another bargain, and be no better off at
the end of ten years than at the beginning. Another
way in which they lost the profits of their labour
was by raising nothing but tobacco, the high price
of which was very tempting, and the cultivation of
which was a monopoly in their hands, as no white
man understood it, or could compete with them at
all. The consequence was, however, that the had

nothing but tobacco to sell, and soon there was rather too much of it in the market, and the price of wheat rose, while their commodity was depressed ; hence they lost all they should have saved, in the profit they gave the trader for his corn and stores.

I saw the effect of these things so clearly, that I could not help trying to make my friends and neighbours see it too ; and I set seriously about the business of lecturing upon the subject of crops, wages, and profit, just as if I had been brought up to it. I insisted on the necessity of their raising their own crops, saving their own wages, and securing the profits of their own labour, using such plain arguments as occurred to me, and were as clear to their comprehension as to mine. I did this very openly ; and, frequently, my audience consisted in part of the very traders whose inordinate profits upon individuals I was trying to diminish, but whose balance of profit would not be ultimately lessened, because they would have so many more persons to trade with, who would be able to pay them a reasonable advance in cash, or its equivalent, on all their purchases. The purse is a tender part of the system ; but I handled it so gently, that the sensible portion of my natural opponents were not, I believe, offended ; while those whom I wished to benefit, saw, for the most part, the propriety of my advice, and took it. At least, there are now great numbers of coloured fugitives, in this region of Canada, who own their farms, are training up their children in true independence, and giving them a good elementary education, who had not taken a

single step towards such a result before I began to
talk to them.

While I remained at Colchester, I became acquainted with a Congregational missionary from
Massachusetts, by the name of Hiram Wilson, who
took an interest in our people, and was disposed to
do what he could to promote the cause of improvement which I had so much at heart. He co-
operated with me in many efforts, and I have been
associated with him for over thirty years. He has
been a faithful friend, and still continues his important labours of love in our behalf. Among other
things, he wrote to a Quaker friend of his, an
Englishman, by the name of James C. Fuller,
residing at Skeneateles, New York, and endeavoured
to interest him in the welfare of our struggling
population.

He succeeded so far, that Mr. Fuller, who was
going on a visit to England, promised to interest his
friends there, to induce them to aid us. He came
back with fifteen hundred dollars which had been
subscribed for our benefit. It was a great question how this sum, which sounded vast to many
of my brethren, should be appropriated. I had my
own decided opinion as to what it was best for us all
to do with it. But, in order to come to a satisfac-
tory conclusion, it was thought expedient to call a
convention of delegates from every settlement of
blacks that was within reach; that all might see
that the ultimate decision was sanctioned by the
disinterested votes of those who were thought by
their companions best able to judge what would meet

the wants of our community.   Mr. Wilson and myself, therefore, called such a convention, to meet in London, Upper Canada, and it was held in June, 1838.

I urged the appropriation of the money to the establishment of a manual-labour school, at which our children could gain those elements of knowledge which are usually taught in a grammar-school. I urged that the boys should be taught, in addition, the practice of some mechanical art, and the girls should be instructed in those domestic arts which are the proper occupation and ornament of their sex ; and that such an establishment would not only train up those who would afterwards instruct others, but that it would gradually enable us to become independent of the white man for our intellectual progress, as we could be for our physical prosperity. It was the more necessary, as in many districts, owing to the insurmountable prejudices of the inhabitants, the children of the blacks were not allowed to share the advantages of the common school. There was some opposition to this plan in the convention ; but in the course of the discussion, which continued for three days, it appeared so obviously for the advantage of all to husband this donation, so as to preserve it for a purpose of permanent utility, that the proposal was, at last, unanimously adopted ; and a committee of three was appointed to select and purchase a site for the establishment. Mr. Wilson and myself were the active members of this committee, and after traversing the country for several months, we could find no place more suitable than that upon which I had had my eye for three or four years, for a permanent settlement, in the town of Dawn.

We therefore bought two hundred acres of fine rich land, on the River Sydenham, covered with a heavy growth of black walnut and white wood, at four dollars the acre. I had made a bargain for two hundred acres adjoining this lot, on my own account; and circumstances favoured me so, that the man of whom I purchased, was glad to let me have them at a large discount from the price I had agreed to pay, if I would give him cash for the balance I owed him. I transferred a portion of the advantage of this bargain to the institution, by selling to it one hundred acres more, at the low price at which I obtained them.

In 1842 I removed with my family to Dawn, and as a considerable number of my friends were soon there about me, and the school was permanently fixed there, as we thought, the future importance of this settlement seemed to be decided. There are many other settlements which are prosperous; indeed, the coloured population is scattered over a territory which does not fall far short of three hundred miles in extent, in each direction, and probably numbers not less than twenty thousand persons in all. We looked to the school, and the possession of landed property by individuals, as two great means by which our oppressed and degraded race could be elevated to enjoy a participation in the blessings of civilisation, whereas they had hitherto been permitted to share only its miseries and vices.

I

My efforts to aid them, in every way in my power, and to procure the aid of others for them, have been constant.   I have made many journeys into New York, Connecticut, Massachusetts, and Maine, in all of which States I have found or made many friends to the cause, as well as personal friends.   I have received many liberal gifts for my people, and experienced much kindness of treatment; but I must be allowed to allude particularly to the donations received from Boston—by which we were enabled to erect a sawmill, and thus to begin in good earnest the clearing of our lands, and to secure a profitable return for the support of our school—as among those which have been most welcome and valuable to us.

Some of the trips I have made, have led to some incidents and observations which must be the theme of a future chapter.

CHAPTER XIX:

LUMBERING OPERATIONS.

INDUSTRIAL PROJECT.—FIND SOME ABLE FRIENDS IN BOSTON.—PROCURE FUNDS AND CONSTRUCT A SAWMILL.—SALES OF LUMBER IN BOSTON.—INCIDENT IN THE CUSTOM HOUSE.

THE land on which we settled in Canada was covered with a beautiful forest of noble trees of various kinds. Our people were accustomed to cut them down and burn them on the ground, simply to get rid of them. Often as I roamed through the forest, I was afflicted at seeing such waste, and longed to devise some means of converting this abundant natural wealth into money, so as to improve the condition of the people.

Full of this subject, I left my home on a journey of observation through the State of New York, and New England. I kept my purposes to myself, not breathing a word of my intentions to any mortal. I found in New York, mills where precisely such logs as those in Canada were sawed into lumber, which I learned commanded large prices. In New England I found a ready market for the black walnut, whitewood, and other lumber, such as abounded and was wasted in Canada.

On reaching Boston, Mass., I made known these

facts and my feelings to some philanthropic gentlemen with whom I had become acquainted. It cannot be improper for me to mention the names of these
gentlemen, who lent so ready an ear to my representations, and placed so much confidence in my
judgment, that they furnished me with the means
of starting what has since proved a very profitable
enterprise.

Rev. Ephraim Peabody introduced me to Samuel
Elliot, Esq., who was kind enough to examine carefully into all my representations, and to draw up a
sketch of them, which was afterwards presented to
Amos Lawrence, Esq., and others. By means of
this, many of the leading gentlemen of Boston contributed about fourteen hundred dollars, to aid me in
this enterprise.

With this money I returned to Canada, and immediately set myself about building a sawmill in
Camden (then Dawn). The improvement in the sur-
rounding section was astonishing. The people began
to labour in earnest, and the progress in clearing and
cultivating the land was cheering.

But after the framework of my mill was completed and covered, my scanty funds were exhausted.
This was a trying time. I had begun the work in
faith, I had expended the money honestly, and to
the best of my judgment, and now should the whole
enterprise fail? I immediately returned to my
Boston friends. Amos Lawrence, H. Ingersoll Bow-
ditch, and Samuel A. Elliot, Esqs., listened to me
again, and gave me to understand that they deemed
me an honest man. They encouraged me in my

business-enterprise, and the approval of such men was like balm to my soul. They endorsed a note for me and put it into the bank, by which I was enabled to borrow, on my own responsibility, about eighteen hundred dollars more. With this I soon completed the mill, stocked it with machinery, and had the pleasure of seeing it in successful operation. I ought here to add, that the mill was not to be my own private property, but to belong to the association, which established an excellent manual-labour school, where many children and youth of both sexes have been educated. The school was well-attended by coloured children, whites, and some Indians.

This enterprise having been completed to a great extent by my own labour and the labour of my own sons, who took charge of the mill, I immediately began to consider how I could discharge my pecuniary obligations. I chartered a vessel, and loaded it with eighty thousand feet of good prime black walnut-lumber, sawed in our mill, and contracted with the captain to deliver it for me at Oswego, N. Y. I entered into a contract there with a party to have it delivered at Boston, but the party having forwarded it to New York, failed to carry it any farther. There great efforts were made to cheat me out of the lumber, but, by the good friendship of Mr. Lawrence, of Boston, who furnished me the means of having it reshipped, I succeeded in bringing the whole eighty thousand feet safely to Boston, where I sold it to Mr. Jonas Chickering for forty-five dollars per thousand feet. The proceeds paid all expenses, and would have cancelled all the debts I had incurred; but my friends insisted that I should retain a part of the funds for future use. After that I brought another large load of lumber by the same route.

The next season I brought a large cargo oy the River St. Lawrence, which came direct to Boston, where, without the aid of any agent or third party whatever, I paid my own duties, got the lumber through the Custom House, and sold it at a handsome profit. A little incident occurred when paying the duties, which has often since afforded me a great deal of amusement. The Fugitive Slave Law had just been passed in the United States, which made it quite an offence to harbour or render aid to a fugitive slave. When the Custom House officer presented his bill to me for the duties on my lumber, I jokingly remarked to him that perhaps he would render himself liable to trouble if he should have dealings with a fugitive slave, and if so, I would relieve him of the trouble of taking my money. "Are you a fugitive slave, sir?" "Yes, sir," said I; "and perhaps you had better not have any dealings with me." "I have nothing to do with that," said the official; "there is your bill. You have acted like a man, and I deal with you as a man." I enjoyed the scene, and the bystanders seemed to relish it, and I paid him the money.

I look back upon the enterprise related in this chapter with a great deal of pleasure, for the mill which was then built, introduced an entire change in the appearance of that section of the country, and in the habits of the people.

CHAPTER XX.

VISIT TO ENGLAND.

DEBT ON THE INSTITUTION.—A NEW PECUNIARY ENTERPRISE.—
LETTERS OF RECOMMENDATION TO ENGLAND.—PERSONAL DIFFI-
CULTIES.—CALLED AN IMPOSTOR.—TRIUMPHANT VICTORY OVER
THESE TROUBLES.

MY interest in the Manual Labour School in Dawn, was the means of my visiting England. Those who have never engaged in such business, can have no idea of the many difficulties connected with so great an enterprise. In spite of all the efforts of the association, a debt of about seven thousand five hundred dollars rested upon it. A meeting of its trustees and friends, in the year 1849, was called to consider its condition, and to devise, if possible, some means for its relief. After a long discussion of the matter, it was finally determined to separate the concern into two departments, and put it under the charge of two parties, the one to take the mill and a certain portion of the land for four years, and to pay all the debts of the institution in that time; and the other party to take the other buildings and land, and to conduct the school.

A certain party was found willing to assume the school. But it was more difficult to find one who would be enterprising enough to take the mill for four years encumbered with a debt of seven thousand five hundred dollars.

At length I concluded to do it, provided that Mr. Peter B. Smith would assume an equal share of the responsibility, and attend to the business of the mill. He readily consented.

I decided to go to England, carry with me some of the best specimens of black walnut-boards our farm would produce and exhibit them in the world's great Industrial Exhibition, then in session at London, and perhaps negotiate there for the sale of lumber. I accordingly left for England, being readily furnished with very complimentary letters of introduction to such men as Thomas Binney, Samuel Gurney, Lord Brougham, Hon. Abbot Lawrence, then American Minister to England, from Rev. John Rolfe, of Toronto, Chief Justice Robinson, Sir Allen McNab, Col. John Prince, Rev. Dr. Duffield, of Detroit, Michigan ; Judge Conant, of the same city ; Hon. Ross Wilkinson, U. S. Judge, residing also in Detroit ; Hon. Charles Sumner and Amos Lawrence, Esq., of Massachusetts. From the gentlemen above mentioned, I had in England a most cordial reception, and was immediately introduced to the very best society in the kingdom.

I regret exceedingly to make any allusions to personal difficulties, or to individuals who have pursued an unjust and unchristian course towards me or others, but I cannot give anything like a correct view of this part of my history, without, at least, a brief allusion to these difficulties.

It was undoubtedly the plan of certain individuals of the party who assumed the care of the school, probably from unworthy sectarian feelings, to obtain entire possession of the property of the association, or certainly, completely to destroy my influence over it and connection with it.

Much to my astonishment, therefore, when I had arrived in England, and had been cordially received by the men above mentioned, and had preached in the pulpits of Rev. Thomas Binney, Baptist Noel, William Brock, James Sherman, George Smith, and Dr. Burns, in London, and had already introduced my enterprise before a portion of the British public, I was confronted by a printed circular, to the following effect : " That one styling himself Rev. Josiah Henson was an impostor, obtaining money under false pretences ; that he could exhibit no good credentials ; that whatever money he might obtain would not be appropriated according to the wish of the donors, and that the said Josiah Henson was an artful, skilful, and eloquent man, and would probably deceive the public." This was a severe blow, but fortunately I had already requested my friends to appoint a committee of twelve persons to examine carefully into the merits of my enterprise, and particularly desired that this committee should appoint a sub-committee of three, and a treasurer, to receive every farthing contributed to me by the public, and to appropriate it only as they should deem proper. This committee had been appointed, and consisted of Samuel Gurney, Samuel Gurney, Junior, Samuel Morley, Esq., George Hitchcock, Esq., Rev. James Sherman, Rev. Thomas

Binney, Rev. John Branch, Eusebius Smith, Esq., John Scobell, Secretary of the British and Foreign Anti-Slavery Society, Lord Ashley (now Earl of Shaftesbury), George Sturge, and Thomas Sturge. The sub-committee of three were, John Scobell, Rev. John Branch, and Eusebius Smith, who appointed Samuel Gurney, Junior, treasurer. Many of the above names are known throughout the world.

When the above attack was made upon me, a meeting of those interested in my cause was called, and my accuser, who was in the country, was requested to meet me face to face.

I believe all the difficulty arose from little petty jealousies, fostered, perhaps, by the unworthy influences of slavery, over the misguided people who were for a time misled by false representations.

We met before a company of English gentlemen, who heard all that my accuser had to say. They asked me for a reply. I simply restated to them the facts I had previously made known. I reminded them that a man who devotes himself to doing good, must and will be misunderstood and have enemies. I called their attention to the misinterpretation of their own motives made by their enemies. I related to them the parable of Christ about the wheat and the tares. My recommendatory letters were re-read —a sufficient reply to the allegation that I was an impostor.

They assured me of their entire confidence and satisfaction; but to be able to clear every aspersion on my character they determined, at their own expense, to send an agent to Canada, to make a full inquiry into the matter, and advised me to accompany him. Accordingly, their agent and myself started for Canada immediately. I had already collected nearly seventeen hundred dollars, which, of course, remained in the hands of the treasurer.

A mass meeting, of all interested in the matter, was called in the institution on the premises. A large assemblage met, and Rev. John Rolfe, of Toronto, presided. A thorough examination into the records of the institution was made. The originator of the slander against me, denied having made it; it was proved upon him, and the whole convention unanimously repudiated the false charges. The agent remained in Canada about three months, and before leaving, sent me a letter, informing me that whenever I should see fit to return to England, I should find in the hands of Amos Lawrence, Esq., of Boston, a draft to defray the expenses of the journey. Accordingly, in the latter part of 1851, I returned.

The ground was now prepared for me, and I reaped an abundant harvest. The whole debt of the institution was cancelled in a few months, when I was recalled to Canada by the fatal illness of my wife. Several very interesting occurrences happened during my stay in England, which I must relate in another chapter.

CHAPTER XXI.

THE WORLD'S FAIR IN LONDON.

I HAVE already mentioned that the first idea which suggested to me the plan of going to England, was to exhibit, at the World's Great Fair, in London, some of the best specimens of our black walnut-lumber, in the hope that it might lead to sales in England. For this purpose, I selected some of the best boards out of the cargo which I had brought to Boston, which Mr. Chickering was kind enough to have properly packed in boxes, and sent to England in the American ship which carried the American products for exhibition. The boards which I selected were four in number, excellent spécimens, about seven feet in length and four feet in width, of beautiful grain and texture. On their arrival in England, I had them planed and perfectly polished, in French style, so that they actually shone like a mirror.

The history of my connection with the World's Fair is a little amusing. Because my boards happened to be carried over in the American ship, the superintendent of the American Department, who was from Boston, insisted that my lumber should be exhibited in the American department. To this I objected. I was a citizen of Canada, my boards were from Canada, and there was an apartment of the building appropriated to Canadian products. I therefore insisted that my boards should be removed from the American department to the Canadian. But, said the American, "You cannot do it. All these things are under my control. You can exhibit what belongs to you if you please, but not a single thing here must be moved an inch without my consent."

This was quite a damper to me. I thought his position was rather absurd, and for the time it seemed impossible to move him or my boards.

A happy suggestion, however, occurred to me. Thought I, if this Yankee wants to retain my furniture, the world shall know who owns it. I accordingly hired a painter to paint in large white letters on the tops of my boards: "THIS IS THE PRODUCT OF THE INDUSTRY OF A FUGITIVE SLAVE FROM THE UNITED STATES, WHOSE RESIDENCE IS DAWN, CANADA." This was done early in the morning. In due time, the American superintendent came around, and found me at my post. The gaze of astonishment with which he read my inscription, was laughable to witness. His face was as black as a thunder-cloud. " Look here, sir," said he. "What, under heaven, have you got up there ?"—"Oh, that is only a little information to let the people know who I am."—"But don't you know better than that ?

Do you suppose I am going to have that insult up
there?" The English gentlemen began to gather
around, chuckling with half-suppressed delight, to
see the wrath of the Yankee. This only added fuel
to the fire. "Well, sir," said he, "do you suppose I
brought that stuff across the Atlantic for nothing?"
—"I never asked you to bring it for nothing. I
am ready to pay you, and have been from the
beginning."—"Well, sir, you may take it away,
and carry it where you please."—"Oh," said I, "I
think, as you wanted it very much, I will not disturb it. You can have it now."—"No, sir; take it
away!"—"I beg your pardon, sir," said I, "when
I wanted to remove it, you would not allow it, and
now, for all me, it shall remain." In the meantime
the crowd enjoyed it and so did I. The result was,
that by the next day, the boards were removed to
their proper place at no expense to me, and no bill
was ever presented to me for carrying the lumber
across the Atlantic.

In that immense exhibition, my humble contribution received its due share of attention. I had
many interesting conversations with individuals
among that almost innumerable multitude from every
nation under heaven. Perhaps my complexion attracted attention, but nearly all who passed, paused
to look at me, and at themselves, as reflected in my
large black walnut mirrors.

Among others, the Queen of England, Victoria,
preceded by her guide, and attended by her cortége,
paused to view me and my property. I uncovered
my head and saluted her as respectfully as I could,

and she was pleased with perfect grace to return my salutation. "Is he indeed a fugitive slave?" I heard her inquire; and the answer was, "He is indeed, and that is his work."

But notwithstanding such pleasant occurrences, the time wore heavily away. The immense crowd, kept in as perfect order as a single family, became wearisome to me, and I was not sorry, as related in a preceding chapter, to go back to Canada, leaving my boards on exhibition.

On returning to England the exhibition was still in progress. There seemed no diminution of the crowd. Like the waters of the great Mississippi, the channel was still full, though the individuals were changed.

But among all the exhibitors from every nation in Europe, and from Asia, America, and the Isles of the Sea, there was not a single black man but myself. There were negroes there from Africa, brought to be exhibited, but no negro-exhibitors but myself. Though my condition was wonderfully changed from what it was in my childhood and youth, yet it was a little saddening to reflect that my people were not more largely represented there. The time will yet come, I trust, when such a state of things will no longer exist.

At the close of the exhibition, on my return to Canada, I received from England a large quarto bound volume containing a full description of all the objects presented at the exhibition, the names of the officers of all the committees, juries, exhibitors, prizes, &c., &c. Among others, I found my own name recorded ; and in addition a bronze medal was awarded to me. I also received a beautiful picture ·of the Queen and royal family, of the size of life, and several other objects of interest.

These testimonials of honour I greatly prize. I fully succeeded in my mission to England, and released myself from the voluntarily-assumed debt in behalf of the manual-labour school. While in England, I was permitted to enjoy some excellent opportunities to witness its best society, which I propose to relate in the following chapter.

CHAPTER XXII.

VISITS TO THE RAGGED SCHOOLS.

SPEECH AT SUNDAY-SCHOOL ANNIVERSARY.—INTERVIEW WITH LORD GREY.—INTERVIEW WITH THE ARCHBISHOP OF CANTERBURY, AND DINNER WITH LORD JOHN RUSSELL, THE GREAT EVENTS OF MY LIFE.

WHILE in England I was frequently called upon to speak at public meetings of various kinds. I was deeply interested in the Ragged School enterprise, and frequently addressed the schools, and also public meetings held in their behalf. I attended most of the great anniversaries held in May, and was called upon to speak at many of them. On several occasions I did what I could, to make known the true condition of slaves, in Exeter Hall and other places. On one occasion, I recollect, an eminent man from Pennsylvania was addressing the anniversary of a Sabbath School Union. He boasted of the great benefits of Sunday schools in the United States, and asserted that all classes indiscriminately enjoyed their blessings. I felt bound to contradict him, and after putting to the speaker a few questions, which he stammeringly answered, I told the immense meeting that in the Southern States, the great body of the coloured people were almost entirely neglected, and in many places they were excluded altogether ; and

K

that in the majority of the Northern States, the great mass of the coloured children were not sought out and gathered into Sunday schools. This created some little storm, but my own personal observation and experience carried conviction to the people.

Being thus introduced to the public, I became well acquainted with many of the leading men of England. Lord Grey made a proposition to me, which, if circumstances had permitted, I should have been glad to have accepted. It was to go to India, and there superintend some great efforts made by the government to introduce the culture of cotton on the American plan. He promised to appoint me to an office, with a good salary. Had it not been for my warm interest in my Canadian enterprise, I should have accepted his proposal.

One of the most pleasing incidents for me now to look back upon, was a long interview which I was permitted to enjoy with the Archbishop of Canterbury. The elevated social position of this man, the highest beneath the crown, is well known to all those acquainted with English society. Samuel Gurney, the noted philanthropist, introduced me, by a note and his family-card, to his grace the archbishop. The latter received me kindly in his palace. I immediately entered into a conversation with him upon the condition of my people, and the plans I had in view. He expressed the strongest interest in me, and after about a half-hour's conversation, he inquired, "At what university, sir, did you graduate?" "I graduated, your grace," said I, in reply, "at the university of adversity." "The university of adversity," said he, looking up with astonishment; "where is that?" I saw his surprise, and explained. "It was my lot, your grace," said I, "to be born a slave, and to pass my boyhood and all the former part of my life as a slave. I never entered a school, never read the Bible in my youth, and received all of my training under the most adverse circumstances. This is what I mean by graduating in the university of adversity." "I understand you, sir," said he. "But is it possible that you are not a scholar?" "I am not," said I. "But I should never have suspected that you were not a liberally educated man. I have heard many negroes talk, but have never seen one that could use such language as you. Will you tell me, sir, how you learned our language?" I then explained to him, as well as I could, my early life; that it had always been my custom to observe good speakers, and to imitate only those who seemed to speak most correctly. "It is astonishing," said the archbishop. "And is it possible that you were brought up ignorant of religion? How did you attain to the knowledge of Christ?" I explained to him, in reply, "that a poor ignorant slave mother had taught me to say the Lord's Prayer, though I did not then know how, truly, to pray." "And how were you led to a better knowledge of the Saviour?" I answered that it was by the hearing of the Gospel preached. He then asked me to repeat the text, and to explain all the circumstances. I told him the text of the first sermon I had heard, was, "He, by the grace of God, tasted death for every man." "A beautiful text was that," said the archbishop, and so affected was he by my simple story, that he shed tears freely.

I had been told by Samuel Gurney that perhaps the archbishop would give me an interview of a quarter of an hour ; I glanced at the clock and found that I had already been there an hour and a half, and arose to depart. He followed me to the door, and begged of me if ever I came to England to call and see him again ; and shaking hands affectionately with me, while the tears trembled in his eyes,* he graciously put into my hands five gold sovereigns, and bade me adieu. I have always esteemed him as a warm-hearted Christian.

Thus ended the interview with the venerable Archbishop Sumner, of England. On my second visit to England, I had an invitation, in company with a large number of Sabbath School teachers, to spend a day in the beautiful grounds of Lord John Russell, then Prime Minister of England. His magnificent park, filled with deer, of varied colours, from all climes, and sleek hares, which the poet Cowper would have envied, with numberless birds, whose plumage rivalled the rainbow in gorgeous colours, together with the choicest specimens of the finny tribe, sporting in their native element, drew from me the involuntary exclamation : " Oh, how different the condition of these happy, sportive, joyful creatures, from what was once my own condition, and what is now the lot of millions of my coloured brethren in America ! " This occupancy of the elegant grounds of England's Prime Minister, for the day, by a party of Sabbath School teachers, was a picnic, with this difference, that, instead of each teacher providing his own cakes, and pies, and fruit, they were furnished by men and women, who were allowed to come on to the grounds, with every variety of choice eatables for sale. After strolling over these charming grounds, enjoying the beautiful scenery, the happy gambols of the brute creation, and the conversation of the many intelligent men and women with whom we came in contact, we were most unexpectedly, at five o'clock, sent for to visit the elegant mansion of the proprietor. There we found what I will call a surprise-party, or at any rate, we were taken by surprise, for three hundred of us were ushered into a spacious dining hall, whose dimensions could not have been less than one hundred feet by sixty, and here were tables, groaning under every article of luxury for the palate, which England could supply, and to this bountiful repast we were all made welcome. I was invited to take the head of the table; I never felt so highly honoured. The blessing was invoked by singing the following verse:

> " Be present at our table, Lord,
> Be here and everywhere adored :
> These creatures bless,
> And grant that we may feast
> In Paradise with Thee ! "

After dinner, various toasts were proposed, on several subjects, and in my humble way I offered the following:

" First to England. Honour to the brave, freedom to the Slave, success to British emancipation. God bless the Queen ! "

Cheers and laughter followed the reading of this toast, succeeded by the usual English exclamations, " *Up, up, up again !* " I again arose and gave, To our most Sovereign Lady, the Queen :

"May she have a long life, and a happy death. May she reign in righteousness, and rule in love !"

And to her illustrious consort, Prince Albert :

"May he have peace at home, pleasure abroad, love his Queen, and serve the Lord !"

Among the distinguished persons who made speeches on this joyous occasion, were Rev. William Brock, Hon. Samuel M. Peto, and the brother-in-law of Mr. Peto, with his accomplished and beautiful lady. Thus ended one of the pleasantest days of my life.

CHAPTER XXIII.

CLOSING UP MY LONDON AGENCY.

THE dinner at Lord John Russell's, as detailed in the previous chapter, was in the month of June, 1852; from that time to the 1st of August, I was busily employed in finishing up all matters connected with my agency, in which I was very successful, having accomplished the objects of my mission. During the month of August, I was engaged in publishing a narrative of incidents in my slave-life, which I had been urgently requested to do by some of the noblest men and women in England. Just as I had completed the work, I received, on the 3rd of September, a letter from my family in Canada, stating that my beloved wife, the companion of my life, the sharer of my joys and sorrows, was at the point of death, and that she earnestly desired me to return immediately, that she might see me once more before she bade adieu to earth. This was a trying hour for me. I was in England, four thousand miles from my home. I was not long in deciding to go home. On the morning of the 4th

of September, having received the letter from home
at four o'clock on the afternoon of the 3rd, I was
on my way from London to Liverpool, and embarked
from Liverpool on the 5th, in the steamer Canada,
bound for Boston. On the 20th of the same
month I arrived at my own Canadian home. Those
who have been placed in similar situations, can
realise what must have been my feelings as I drew
near my humble dwelling. I had heard nothing
since the information contained in the letter which
reached me at Liverpool. I knew not whether my
dear wife, the mother of my children, she who had
travelled with me, sad, solitary, and footsore, from
the land of bondage, who had been to me a kind,
affectionate, and dutiful wife for forty years, was
still alive, or whether she had entered into her rest.

A merciful Father had, however, kindly prolonged
her life, and we were permitted once more to meet.
And oh! such a meeting! I was met in the yard
by four of my daughters, who rushed to my arms,
delighted at my unexpected return. They begged
me not to go in to see mother, until they should
first go and prepare her for it, thinking very wisely
that the shock would be too great for her poor
shattered nerves to bear. I consented that they
should precede me. They gradually prepared her
mind for our meeting. When I went to her bedside, she received and embraced me with the calmness and fortitude of a Christian, and even chided
me for the strong emotions of sorrow which I found
it utterly impossible to suppress. I found her perfectly calm and resigned to the will of God, awaiting

with Christian firmness the hour for her summons. She was rejoiced to see me once more, while at the same time she said that perhaps she had done wrong in allowing me to leave England when my business-prospects were so flattering. I told her that I was more than satisfied, that I was truly thankful to my Heavenly Father for granting us this interview, no matter what the pecuniary sacrifice might be. We talked over our whole past life as far as her strength would permit, reviewing the many scenes of sorrow and trouble, as well as the many bright and happy days of our pilgrimage, until exhausted nature sought repose, and she sunk into a quiet sleep.

The day following she revived ; my return seemed to inspire her with the hope that possibly she might again be restored to health. It was not, however, so to be ; but God in His mercy granted her a reprieve, and her life was prolonged a few weeks. I thus had the melancholy satisfaction of watching day and night by her bed of languishing and pain, and was permitted to close her eyes when the final summons came. She blessed me, and blessed her children, commending us to the ever-watchful care of that Saviour who had sustained her in so many hours of trial ; and finally, after kissing me and each one of the children, she passed from earth to heaven without a pang or a groan, as gently as the falling to sleep of an infant on its mother's breast.

> " Who would not wish to die like those
>   Whom God's own Spirit deigns to bless ?
> To sink into that soft repose,
>   Then wake to perfect happiness ? "

I can truly and from an overflowing heart say, that she was a sincere and devoted Christian, a faithful and kind wife to me, even to the day of her death arranging all our domestic matters, in such a manner as to contribute as largely as possible to my comfort and happiness.

CHAPTER XXIV.

MY BROTHER'S FREEDOM.

AM I MY BROTHER'S KEEPER?—EFFORTS TO SECURE HIS FREE-
DOM.—ATTEMPTS TO RAISE THE MONEY.—UNION OF HIS FAMILY.

I RECEIVED numerous tokens of regard from many
philanthropic gentlemen while I was in London, which I shall never forget; but I was particularly touched by the special kindness of Samuel
Morley, Esq., and George Hitchcock, Esq., of St.
Paul's Churchyard. These two gentlemen invited
me to dine with them every day at half-past one.
I gratefully accepted their invitation, and dined
alternately with these gentlemen, always receiving
a very warm welcome from them. The spirit of
manhood, one of the strongest elements of my mind,
was in no instance wounded, for I was invariably
received and entertained as a respected guest. One
day I was sitting at Mr. Morley's table, and was
about to partake of his bountiful supply of nourish-
ing food, when suddenly my mind reverted to the
past. I remembered the trying scenes of my eventful life, and that my only brother was still bound in
the iron chains of slavery, deprived of all the comforts of life, dragging out an abject, miserable existence, while I was surrounded with luxuries, and

sitting at the sumptuous table of one of the first men in the kingdom. I could almost hear the clanking of his chains, and, in my mind's eye, see him with scarcely a crust of bread to satisfy his hunger, or a glass of water to quench his thirst. I was so forcibly impressed with my vision, that I rose from the table without eating a mouthful of food.

Struck with my unusual appearance, for I had always been cheerful and happy, Mr. Morley said, " What is the matter, Josiah? Has anything occurred to disturb your peace of mind?"

At first I could not control my emotions sufficiently, to reply. He added, " Come, come, Josiah, do help yourself and make yourself at home."

Soon I summoned the courage to tell him the cause of my agitation, and asked him " to excuse me from eating my dinner on that day, for I had no appetite."

I then and there resolved in my own mind, that as soon as I returned to America, I would make every possible effort to secure to my brother the blessed freedom I enjoyed.

Slavery had no power to eradicate the social ties that bound the different members of a family together, and though families were often torn asunder, yet memory generally kept the affections warm and abiding.

I had made several efforts to induce my brother to run away previous to my going to England. Mr. William L. Chaplain, of New York, saw him in his southern home, and tried to induce him to take the underground railroad—that is, to run away. But he found my brother's mind so demoralised or stultified by slavery, that he would not risk his life in the attempt to gain his freedom, and he informed me of this fact. Still I could not rest contented, and Mr. Chaplain promised to make another effort, as he intended to visit the neighbourhood again. He laboured with my brother the second time, with no good result, and then he endeavoured to assist Mr. Toomb's slaves, who had resolved to escape from Georgia to Canada. Mr. Chaplain was detected, and thrown into prison to await a trial. He was released on bail, three times the amount of the value of the slaves. The Hathaways, benevolent Quakers of Farmington, New York, Asa B. Smith, and William R. Smith, his son, of the same town, paid the bail, which they desired Mr. Chaplain to forfeit, as they knew that the result of a trial would be that he would be hung. I will here add that the Smiths had to sell their farms, and were pecuniarily ruined for the time, and it is with pleasure that I make this record of their generosity in the Anti-Slavery cause.

On my return to Canada, the release of my brother was my uppermost thought. Whenever I have adopted the language of the prodigal son, who said, "I will arise, and go to my father," —that is, when I have uttered in my heart the words, "God helping me, I will,"—I have somehow had the ability to accomplish my undertaking. Though I may have been obliged to change my plans and course of action, and pursue others more feasible, yet, ultimately, the end has been most

marvellously attained. All my previous plans to
rescue my brother had failed, but I was not at all
disposed to relinquish the project. By the aid of
friends, I learned that the mistress to whom my
brother belonged would give him his freedom-papers
for 400 dollars, and I concluded that I must raise
550 dollars, or about £110, so that I should be able
to take him to my home in Canada. I consulted
some of the Anti-Slavery friends in Boston, particularly Amos Lawrence, Esq., and they agreed to pub-
lish the story of my life, as I had suggested to them,
that I might be able, from its sale, to raise a sufficient sum of money to buy my brother's freedom. I
took a package of the books on my back and travelled
in the New England States, and succeeded in interesting the people, so that I was enabled to raise the
money I required. Then, through the negotiation
of Mr. Charles C. Berry, cashier of the City Bank
in Boston, Massachusetts, who had friends at the
South, I joyfully sent the ransom. Soon my brother
came from Maryland to Baltimore; thence by sea to
Boston, where I met him and took him to my home
in Canada, and kept him there for fifteen years.
When President Lincoln's Proclamation of Emancipation gave freedom to all the slaves in America,
my brother's eldest son came to Canada to see his
father, and the meeting would have done President
Lincoln's heart good if he had witnessed it.

The son went back and remained with his mother
and brothers for three years. Then he came to
Canada to take my brother to rejoin his wife and
family in New Jersey; for after the Emancipation

Act was enforced, my brother's mistress removed from Maryland to New Jersey, where her husband bought a large dairy-farm. She had in vain endeavoured to suit herself with ordinary white servants. Then she persuaded my brother to bring his family to her farm, and they have remained with her to this day as hired servants, receiving excellent wages for their faithful services. My brother's eldest son superintends her dairy, and is the head-man, in whom great confidence is placed. My brother is now ninety-one years of age, and is the only living relative I have, excepting my wife and children.

CHAPTER XXV.

MRS. STOWE'S CHARACTERS.

MY VISIT TO MRS. STOWE.—WHY I AM CALLED "UNCLE TOM."
—HER INTEREST IN MY LIFE-STORY.—HER FAMOUS BOOK.—IS
IT AN EXAGGERATION?—MRS. STOWE'S KEY.

AFTER my successful visit to England, I travelled
in Canada, and in Maine, New Hampshire,
Vermont, Massachusetts, Connecticut, and Rhode
Island. In all these states I was cordially welcomed
as a speaker in the pulpits of the Congregationalists,
Presbyterians, Methodists, Baptists, and Universal-
ists. I held many meetings, and discussed the
subject of slavery in all its bearings on society. At
that time, slavery was considered to be a permanent
institution of the South, and it was supposed that
nothing but an earthquake would have the power to
break up the foundations of the system. It is a
mistaken idea that the majority of the slaveholders
would have sold their slaves if the government had
offered to buy them. They liked the system, had
grown up with it, and were not disposed to part
with it without a struggle. Anti-slavery ideas were
not popular at the South, nor generally at the North.
On this account, those who had sufficient moral
courage to discuss the merits and demerits of the

system, were accustomed to hold meetings and conventions for this purpose. I was constantly travelling and doing all I could to help to change the public sentiment at the North. I was in the vicinity of Andover, Mass., where Mrs. Harriet Beecher Stowe resided. She sent for me and my travelling companion, Mr. George Clark, a white gentleman, who had a fine voice for singing, and usually sang at my meetings to add to their interest. We went to Mrs. Stowe's house, and she was deeply interested in the story of my life and misfortunes, and had me narrate its details to her. She said she was glad it had been published, and hoped it would be of great service, and would open the eyes of the people to the enormity of the crime of holding men in bondage. She manifested so much interest in me, that I told her about the peculiarities of many slaveholders, and the slaves in the region where I had lived for forty-two years. My experiences had been more varied than those of the majority of slaves, for I was not only my master's overseer, but a market-man for twenty-five years in the market at Washington, going there to sell the produce from my master's plantation.

Soon after, Mrs. Stowe's remarkable book, " Uncle Tom's Cabin," was published, and circulated in all parts of America, and read openly at the North, stealthily at the South. Many thought that her statements were exaggerations. She then published the key to the book to prove that it was impossible to exaggerate the enormities of slavery, and she therein gave many parallel cases, and referred to my pub-

L

lished life-story, as an exemplification of the truth
of the character of her Uncle Tom. From that time
to the present, I have been called " Uncle Tom," and
I feel proud of the title. If my humble words in any
way inspired that gifted lady to write such a plaintive story that the whole community has been
touched with pity for the sufferings of the poor
slave, I have not lived in vain; for I believe that
her book was the beginning of the glorious end. It
was a wedge that finally rent asunder that gigantic
fabric with a fearful crash.

Though she made her hero die, it was fit that she
did this to complete her story; and if God had not
given to me a giant's constitution, I should have
died over and over again long before I reached
Canada. I regard it as one of the most remarkable
features of my life that I have rallied after so many
exposures to all kinds of hardships. I am grateful
to God for His abundant mercies to me in bringing
me out of Egypt into the promised land, and I hope
to be His faithful servant to my dying hour.

The white slaves, George Harris, and his wife
Eliza, were my particular friends. George Harris,
whose real name is Lewis Clark, is about three parts
white. He has travelled and lectured with me in
the New England States. He is a very ingenious
and intelligent man, as Mrs. Stowe represented him.
He and his wife lived in Canada for a long time
after their escape from slavery, and finally moved to
Oberlin, Ohio, to educate their children, for there
is still a great prejudice, in certain localities of
Canada, with regard to admitting children who

have one drop of black blood in their veins, into the schools where white children are taught; yet the coloured people of those districts pay their proportion of taxes and school-rates.

Many people thought that Mrs. Stowe's interesting description of Eliza was a great exaggeration, and that it was impossible for a slave woman to escape in such a manner. That Mrs. Stowe had a real incident for her character will be evident from the following quotation from the published "Reminiscences of Levi Coffin," in which he gives the truthful version of this thrilling incident, as told him by the woman herself:

"She said she was a slave from Kentucky, the property of a man who lived a few miles back from the Ohio River, below Ripley, Ohio. Her master and mistress were kind to her, and she had a comfortable home, but her master got into some pecuniary difficulty, and she found that she and her only child were to be separated. She had buried two children, and was doubly attached to the one she had left, a bright, promising child, over two years old. When she found that it was to be taken from her, she was filled with grief and dismay, and resolved to make her escape that night, if possible. She watched her opportunity, and when darkness had settled down, and all the family had retired to sleep, she started with her child in her arms and walked straight toward the Ohio River. She knew that it was frozen over at that season of the year, and hoped to cross without difficulty on the ice; but when she reached its banks at daylight she found that the ice had broken up and was slowly drifting in large cakes. She ventured to go to a house near by, where she was kindly received and permitted to remain through the day. She hoped to find some way to cross the river the next night, but there seemed little prospect of any one being able to cross in safety, for during the day the ice became more broken and dangerous to cross. In the evening she discovered that pursuers were near the house, and with desperate courage she determined to cross the river or perish in the attempt. Clasping her child in her arms, she darted out of the back door and ran toward the river, followed by her pursuers, who had just dismounted from their horses when they caught sight of her. No fear or thought of personal danger entered Eliza's mind, for she felt that she would rather be drowned than be captured and separated from her child. Clasping her babe to her bosom with her left arm, she sprang on to the first cake of ice, then from that to another and another. Sometimes the cake she was on would sink beneath her weight, then she would slide her child on to the next cake, pull herself on with her hands, and so continue her hazardous journey. She became wet to the waist with ice-water, and her hands were benumbed with cold, but as she made her way from one cake of ice to another, she felt that surely the Lord was preserving and upholding her, and that nothing could harm her.

"When she reached the Ohio side near Ripley, she was completely exhausted and almost breathless. A man who had been standing on the bank watching her progress with amazement, and expecting every moment to see her go down, assisted her up the bank. After she had recovered her strength a little, he directed her to a house on the hill in the outskirts of the town. She made her way to the place, and was kindly received and cared for. It was not considered safe for her to remain there during the night, so, after resting awhile, and being provided with food and dry clothing, she was conducted to a station on the underground railroad, a few miles farther from the river. The next night she was forwarded on from station to station to our house in Newport, where she arrived safely and remained several days.

"Other fugitives arrived in the meantime, and Eliza and her child were sent with them by the Greenville branch of the underground railroad to Sandusky, Ohio. They reached that place in safety, and crossed the lake to Canada, locating finally at Chatham, Canada West."

Eliza died in Oberlin this year, but her husband is still an active, enterprising man. His brother's complexion is so nearly white, that it is almost impossible for any one, who is not acquainted with his history, to perceive that he has any coloured blood. He is in the Custom House in Boston, Mass.

There was on our plantation a negro girl, Dinah, who was as near like Mrs. Stowe's Topsy as two peas in a pod. Dinah was clear-witted, as sharp and cunning as a fox, but she purposely acted like a fool, or idiot, in order to take advantage of her mistress. When the latter said, "Dinah, go and do your work," she would reply with a laugh, "Yes, yes; when I get ready;" or, "Go, do it yourself." Sometimes she would scream out, "I won't; that's a lie—catch me if you can;" and then she would take to her heels and run away. She was so queer and funny in her ways, that she was constantly doing all kinds of odd things, but escaped the whipping that other slaves, who did not behave half so badly, had received daily, because her mistress thought she was an idiot.

There was a gentleman, Mr. St. Clair Young, who lived in the neighbourhood of my old home. He was as kind-hearted as Mrs. Stowe's St. Clair. Soon after I left the district, I learned that he became a converted man, gave his slaves their freedom, sold his land, moved into Indiana, and preached as a Methodist minister.

It is a fact, that as soon as the conscience of a slaveholder was aroused, he was obliged to give up his slaves or his religious convictions; for these were so antagonistic they could not agree. Mr. St. Clair Young had a sweet little girl who could easily have been the original of precious little Eva. The children of slaveholders were often kind-hearted, good-tempered, and were genial companions during their childhood, before they were old enough to exercise authority. Then, under the influence of their circumstances, slavery would often turn the mildest disposition into a cross one, the same as thunder will turn sweet milk.

Bryce Litton, who broke my arms and maimed me for life, would stand very well for Mrs. Stowe's cruel Legree. Litton was the most tyrannical, barbarous man I ever saw, and I have good reason to know that his revengeful and malicious spirit would have led him to perform the most cruel acts. He lived a miserable life, like a hog, and died like a dog a few years after I left that part of the country. He was universally detested even among slaveholders, for when an overseer far exceeded the bounds of what they termed humanity, he was a marked man, his society was avoided, and his career was by no means a pleasant one. Even slaveholders, like thieves, had a certain creed of honour.

Mrs. Stowe's book is not an exaggerated account of the evils of society. The truth has never been half-told; the story would be too horrible to hear. I could fill this book with cases that have come under my own experience and observation, by which I could prove that the slaveholder could and did break every one of the ten commandments with impunity. A slave was not allowed to testify against a white man in a court of justice, hence he had to bear all the cruelties his master was pleased to inflict. I could give statements of facts that would appal a generous and kind-hearted soul.

CHAPTER XXVI.

THE MANUAL LABOUR SCHOOL AT DAWN.

TROUBLES.—MISPLACED CONFIDENCE.—EYES OPENED.—LAWSUIT.—
WILBERFORCE UNIVERSITY.

DIFFICULTIES had arisen in the management of the Manual Labour Institution at Dawn, before I visited England in 1851. Debts had accumulated, and I had pledged myself to take the saw-mill and part of the land, and clear off the debts as I have before explained. The school was established with the express idea that it was not to promulgate sectarianism. But those who had obtained control over it, were inclined to drift it into a particular sect. I opposed this, and hence incurred their disapprobation. Soon after I visited England, and began to raise a fund for the benefit of the school; but, as I before stated, the dominant party attempted to counteract my efforts by slandering me. My committee in London proposed that a gentleman should visit Canada, and ascertain the facts respecting my personal character. Mr. Samuel Morley suggested that I should go to Canada with the gentleman. He said, " If things are as you say, Josiah, we will provide a way for you to return, and you can then finish your work here. But if you are an impostor, as your enemies have represented, you will then be at home with your family; you will not want to come back, and we shall not want to see you. If it were proved you were here getting money on false pretences, nothing would save you from being sent to Van Diemen's Land."

When we reached Canada, there was a convention called on the premises where the school was located; careful inquiries were made, and no charges were found against me. After this English gentleman had ascertained all the particulars, he returned to England, made a favourable report to my committee, and remained in England for a year or two.

Before he left America, he arranged with Amos Lawrence, Esq., of Boston, that I was to go to England when I was ready, and deposited the money with him for my passage. Accordingly, in the winter of 1851, the same year, I was back in England; I finished my work, raised about £1,000 for the school, and left this money, which was sufficient to defray all the debts of the school, in the hands of the treasurer, Mr. Gurney, of London. The English gentleman told the trustees of the school at Dawn, " that the spot could be made the brightest spot in the garden of the Lord, if there were only an efficient manager at its head to control it." All but one of the trustees agreed to assign the institution to him to manage. He promised to clear it from debt, and represented to the trustees " that the committee in London whom I had selected, would be responsible for him, or would aid him in placing the school on a permanent foundation, and in making it a glorious moral lighthouse, a beacon whose illumination should be perpetual."

This looked reasonable, and I agreed with the trustees when they conferred upon him the assignment, for I knew that he was respected in London, had been sent to the West Indies to inquire into the condition of slavery there, and that his reports had helped to secure the emancipation of the slaves in the West Indies.

He presented the case to the committee in London, and when he told them he expected they would endorse him, Samuel Morley said, "We did not authorise you to represent that we would shoulder the responsibility of the school, and we cannot do it." It was decided that the committee would be interested in the welfare of the school, but that they would not incur any pecuniary risks for it.

In about two years the gentleman returned to Canada, and took with him the funds I had raised for the school debts. He bought up the debts, giving to some 62 cents in the dollar, to others the full amount. Then, his family being with him, he took possession of the premises, and the charge of the institution in earnest. He said, "I am going to renovate this place, 'de novo.'" I shall never forget those words, they sounded so grandly to my ears.

I soon found he intended to commence at the beginning. I had great faith in his integrity, and believed every word he uttered, and at that time would have pledged myself to carry out his ideas to the uttermost. As the land was in splendid condition, he probably anticipated having by-and-by a model farm, which would bring a large annuity.

It is my candid opinion that, in the beginning, he intended to benefit the coloured race, and to have a splendid school which should be the pride of the neighbourhood. If he had been a practical instead of a theoretical farmer, he doubtless would have accomplished those blessed results. He soon began to buy the most expensive cattle in the market, at fancy prices, and without any reference to the fact that he had not sufficient fodder to feed them after he had them in his stables. He also bought expensive farming utensils to work the farm scientifically, and then pulled down the school-buildings, as they were too primitive to suit his magnificent ideas, and he promised to erect more substantial and commodious buildings. I upheld him in all these suggestions, for I had a kind of respect for the man that almost amounted to veneration.

At his request, I often went to market with him, and he generally asked my judgment about the fine cattle that he was constantly adding to his stock. I sometimes ventured to suggest that they would require a great amount of grain during the long Canadian winter. But he invariably declined to take my advice in this respect, and I concluded he knew what he was doing, and must have had experience, or he would not have pursued such a reckless course.

One year passed away, and there were no school buildings and no school. Our people said, "Surely he will commence building next year." The second

year passed away, and again I silenced the question-
ings and murmurings; for I still had confidence in
his integrity of purpose.   The third year passed, and
then the coloured people began to tell me " I was in
league with him, and that in some way he and I
were gaining pecuniary advantages from the cultivation of that splendid tract of three hundred acres of
land on the Sydenham River."

By-and-by his finances became involved, and he
borrowed of me several hundred dollars to meet his
bills, and the fourth year passed; still there was no
school.   He supported his family and his brother-in-
law's family from the farm that belonged to our
coloured people.   True, the family of his brother-in-
law, from their straitened circumstances, frequently
came to my house for food, and my wife gave them
the best we had.   The fifth, sixth, seventh, eighth,
and ninth year passed, and we had no school, and not
an individual could make any change.   He had no
title to the land, so he had no power to sell this, and
it was a most fortunate thing.   I had repeatedly said
to him, " The people are growling."   He replied,
" Let them growl."   He invariably refused to discuss the question.   At length, when nine years had
passed, I began to doubt the man's intentions, and I
thought I would have a serious conversation with
him on the subject, and ascertain what he proposed
doing.   I said to him as politely as I could, " The
people about here are beginning to talk very hard
about you and myself, and I do not want to let them
have any cause to think ill of us.   If you will be so
kind as to give me some intimation when you propose

to commence the school-buildings I can satisfy them."
He curtly replied, "When I get ready; when I
please." I said, meekly, "It is quite unfortunate for
me, for my honour is impeached, as I have always
defended you."

"What's your honour to me? I don't care what
they say." He added, in a very dignified manner,
"I did not come here for the coloured people to
dictate to me."

I replied, "If you really do not intend to build us
a school, you ought to leave the farm, and let us
manage for ourselves."

With some excitement he said, "Pay me what I
have expended during the many years I have tried
to make this place meet its expenses, and I will go
at once."

The scales fell from my eyes; I saw through the
man's motives. I went to the coloured people and
told them, sadly, "that I had been greatly deceived,
that we should never have a school until we gained
possession of the property, and that if I had a power
of attorney to act for them I would consult an able
lawyer, and ascertain what could be done." A convention of the coloured people of the region was
called. I was given by them the power of attorney
to examine the subject and act for them. I went
immediately to London, Canada, and laid the case
before Lawyer Wilson, since made a judge, and
Lawyer McKenzie, two eminent lawyers. They
promised to weigh the matter very carefully, and to
let me know the result. In about three months they
sent me word "that if I could find two substantial

men, one coloured and one white, who owned free-
hold property unencumbered, and were willing to
pledge themselves to pay the costs, that they would
undertake the case." They said " I must keep in the
background, while the two men should be the osten-
sible ' relators.' " I found the men that same night,
and pledged myself to them " that I would pay the
costs if they would allow their names to be used."
The attorney-general brought the suit for non-fulfil-
ment of trusts and for maladministration of the affairs
of the school. A clever lawyer of Toronto defended
the gentleman, and the war commenced in earnest.
In the beginning I paid two hundred dollars, and
borrowed money from time to time by mortgaging,
first one house and lot, then three houses and
lots, then re-mortgaged them, then sold several lots
to pay the mortgages, then re-mortgaged, and was
constantly called upon to pay disbursements to the
lawyers. It was an anxious, perplexing period, for
the case was taken from court to court, till *seven*
years had elapsed, when at last, wearied and exhausted, the lawyer offered to give it up as a non-
suit if his expenses during these seven years could be
paid. To this we all agreed, and the important case
was decided in our favour. Then the Court of
Chancery appointed a new board of trustees, granted
a bill to incorporate the institution as the Wilberforce University, also the power to sell the land,
which brought about 30,000 dollars, £6,000, in cash,
with a stipulation that the University should be
erected on a plot of ground in the same county. The
town of Chatham, Canada, was selected, and for four

years the school has been *self-sustaining,* and has been attended by many pupils.

Thus ended seven years of perplexity and excitement. During them I learned many practical lessons.

In the beginning of the contest the gentleman left the premises, but installed his son as master over them. I had leased a plot of ground on the school-farm, and had ploughed it for several years. When this young gentleman heard that my men were ploughing the ground, he sent word to them "to be off his premises." I said to my men, "Go to your ploughing to-morrow morning, and I will be there to sustain you."

The next morning my men began their work. Soon the young gentleman appeared on the spot with several of his men. He commanded mine "to leave at once." I was at hand, and said, "I leased this land from your father, and as long as he retains the possession of the whole farm I have a legal right to work this plot, and I shall defend that right."

He mildly said, "Why, Mr. Henson, is that you? I thought you were a praying man, not a fighting man?"

I replied, "When it is necessary I can fight, as I have done for Canada when she was in trouble. I intend to respect the rights of others, and they must respect mine." He soon became angry; first came words, then blows. I could not prevent him from bruising his head several times against my heavy walking-stick, which I held before me to ward off the blows he attempted to level at me. When he was tired of that kind of play, he went off muttering a threat, "that he would have a writ served upon me immediately." I at once had my fastest horse harnessed to my waggon, and rode off to the nearest magistrate accompanied by a constable. The magistrate readily gave me a writ for the young gentleman. When we were returning we met him within a mile from the railroad-station. He had intended to go and see his father, and then have a summons out for me. The constable alighted, touched him on the shoulder, and said, "You are my prisoner, in the name of the Queen, for assault and battery on Josiah Henson on his own premises."

He was crestfallen and very angry, especially when he was obliged to walk between ten and fifteen miles to Dresden to the court to have his trial. His lawyer removed the trial from one court to another, till at London, Canada, he was compelled to pay costs and a bonus to end the suit. He gave me no further trouble, for he perceived that I had a practical knowledge of the common laws of the country. This incident shows how important it was for the coloured people to be able to defend their natural and inalienable rights after they became freemen and citizens of Canada.

CHAPTER XXVII.

IDOLS SHATTERED.

As so many of my friends have been interested in the history of the sawmill that was erected on our school-premises, a few words about its fate may be appreciated. It was a great undertaking to secure the money necessary to purchase the materials for the mill, and the building of it, and a great responsibility to work it successfully. It would have continued to have been a very profitable investment, as it was at first, had it been properly managed; for the River Sydenham is navigable for vessels, and we could send the lumber by water to Detroit, or to almost any part of the United States.

Though there was no school on the premises, the mill was leased to a man who employed forty or fifty men, and they worked faithfully, sawed many thousand feet of lumber, and the lumber was shipped from time to time to different ports. After several prosperous years there came a period of depression, simply because the man who leased the mill did not attend to his business carefully. At length he had a lot of timber sawed, filled three vessels with it, and these sailed for some unknown port. The man

M

disappeared and left his workmen in a starving condition, with their wages in arrears. He gave out the word that he was going off to lay in supplies for the future. The men had no money and could not procure the necessaries of life. They waited till they were convinced their master did not intend to return; then they vented their angry and revengeful feelings on the mill itself, and tore up even its foundations. Thus they ruthlessly destroyed this valuable building, the establishment of which had cost me so many anxious hours, and had proved to be such a valuable piece of property in my hands. When it was gone, I felt as if I had parted with an old idolised friend.

Though Canada was the land of freedom to the fugitive slaves, yet they met with so much prejudice at first, on account of their colour, that it was with difficulty they could procure the common comforts of life. When they endeavoured to have their corn ground they found it no easy matter. A man would often walk three and four miles with two or three bushels on his shoulders, through paths in which the mud was knee-deep, leave his corn at the mill, and then go repeatedly after it in vain; he would be put off with a variety of excuses till he was quite discouraged, and would conclude that it was almost useless for him to raise any grain; and yet there was no other way for him to have a bit of bread or corn-cake. I was tired of hearing these complaints, which became real grievances, and without having a spare dollar in my pocket, I determined that, as the only remedy was to have a grist-mill, independently of any already established, I would erect one and help the coloured people out of their difficulties.

Accordingly I went to Boston, Mass., among my devoted friends, and told them of the necessities of the case, and by their generous help, which, thank God, has never failed me in an hour of need, I soon collected 5,000 dollars, or £1,000, obtained a plan, arranged for its building, introduced steam-power to work it, and in a short time we ground the corn for the entire neighbourhood, and this venture was a decided success.

When the lawsuit commenced, I did not wish to have any trouble with the young gentleman who was placed on the school-premises, about the grist-mill, which I had rented to a man. A short time previously I, therefore, proposed to sell the mill, as it belonged to me personally ; but I agreed to move it from the grounds of the institution, as I had no lease of the land on which it was built, so I was obliged to resort to stratagem to accomplish my purpose. My son-in-law was the miller, and acceded to my proposition, which was that twenty men should be secreted in the mill one Sunday night, and as soon as the hour of midnight had struck, these men should carefully take down the mill and remove every vestige, foundation, engine, and timber, a short distance on to the road, which was the common highway. By ten o'clock on Monday morning the mill had vanished, as if by magic, from its old resting-place, and by noon it was carried off, in ten or twelve teams that were in readiness, to Dresden. It was erected speedily, and it remains there to this day, in splendid working order.

·CHAPTER XXVIII.

FUGITIVE SLAVES ENLISTING IN THE STATES.

TAKING UP ARMS FOR MY COUNTRY.—CIVIL WAR IN AMERICA.—
RISK OF IMPRISONMENT FOR SEVEN YEARS.—SPECIAL PROVI-
DENCE SAVES ME.

DURING the Canadian rebellion I was appointed a captain to the 2nd Essex Company of Coloured Volunteers. Though I could not shoulder a musket, I could carry a sword. My company held Fort Maldon from Christmas till the following May, and also took the schooner Ann and captured all it carried, which were three hundred arms, two cannons, musketry, and provisions for the rebel troops. This was a fierce and gallant action, and it did much towards breaking up the rebel party, for they could not obtain provisions while we held the fort, which we continued to do till we were relieved by the colonel of the 44th Regiment from England. The coloured men were willing to help defend the government that had given them a home when they had fled from slavery.

My sword had been turned into a ploughshare. When the civil war in America broke out, somehow the coloured people in Canada had an idea that the result of it would be the abolition of slavery. If I could have carried a gun, I would have gone personally, but I thought it was my duty to talk to the people. I told them "that the young and able-bodied ought to go into the field like men, that they should stand up to the rack, and help the government." My oldest son, Tom, who was in California, enlisted on a man-of-war in San Francisco, and I suppose he must have been killed, as I have not heard from him since that time.

My son-in-law, Wheeler, enlisted in Detroit. I advised the people, in general terms, to do the same, and said that if any of them wished to go to enlist early, so as to secure the bounty offered, I would provide for their families till they could send the bounty-money to them. A number went, and some lost their bounty-money through "sharpers" lying in wait for them. So I proposed to go with a second lot, that they need not be annoyed in this way. There was one man, named John Alexander, who had decided to be of this second company. I therefore sent some pork and clothing from the stores to his wife and family, as they were poor. At the last he gave me the slip, and during my absence he traitorously and untruthfully declared "that I had tried to induce him and others to enlist." He even testified to this statement before a magistrate, and my wife telegraphed to me "to remain in Boston and not return, for a writ was ready to take me as soon as I appeared in Dresden, and if the charge was proved, the penalty, by the Foreign Enlistment Act, would be seven years' imprisonment." At first I thought I would remain away till the excitement had subsided. Then I reflected that what I had done was for the cause of Christ, and with good motives; that the war was a righteous war; that the coloured people ought to take some part in it. I said to one of my companions, "God helping me, I will not run away when I have done no wrong."

I soon returned to Dresden, and rode in a waggon to my own door in the most public manner; for I was not ashamed to be seen. This was on a Thursday afternoon about four o'clock. My family were highly excited, and, with tears in their eyes, begged me to go away; but I said, "I must remain and have this slander cleared up publicly, as the whole community had been discussing it." The next morning, Friday, before seven o'clock, the constable, an old friend, came to my home. I was sitting on the fence talking to my son-in-law. The constable said, pleasantly, "Good morning, Mr. Henson; have you any potatoes to sell?" "Good morning," I answered. "Yes, sir, I have some." "I should like to buy a few if you can spare any." "How many do you want?" "Ten or fifteen bushels." "I can spare one hundred bushels." "Oh, I do not want so many." "Very well; I suppose it is only one good black potato about my size that you want, and you can have it if you will come and get it."

He at once came forward, put his hand on my shoulder, and said, "Mr. Henson, you are my prisoner in the name of the Queen. Here is a writ for you."

"All right, Bill." His name was William Nellis.

"Let me have a bit of breakfast, and then you can have me." We went into the house, where my wife and children were crying. I invited the constable to eat, but he declined, saying he had eaten his breakfast. We talked for half an hour. Then I took my hat and said to him, "I am ready; how are we going? The writ says you must take me."

The constable said, "If you will have your horse and waggon prepared, I'll pay for it." "I will do no such a thing; you must take me, and if you have no other way, go get a wheelbarrow, for I will not walk with you." He argued with me for an hour or two, till it was nearly noon. Then I said, "You can go your way when you like, and you may tell the squire I will soon be there."

I found that two clever magistrates had arranged everything before I came home. I was not allowed to make a defence or to have a lawyer to plead my case. One of the magistrates was prejudiced against me on account of the interest I had taken in the suit against the school-trustees; the other, Squire Terrace, was my friend. But both were obliged to decide legally, and if they had agreed as to the interpretation of the law, there would have been no opportunity for me to appeal from the magistrate's court. They did not agree, and the case was referred to the next magistrate. When he had heard the statements, he could not decide, and it was proposed to consult the county attorney, Mr. McLean, of Chatham, who was a friend of mine. I had worked faithfully for his grandfather, and was esteemed by the family as a man who conscientiously kept his word, and tried to discharge every known duty. Mr. McLean said, "I am surprised to find these charges against Mr. Henson. He is a common-sense man, and knows the laws better than the majority of the people. There must be a screw loose somewhere in this affair. If what John Alexander has declared on oath be true, nothing will prevent Mr. Henson from seven years' imprisonment in Kingston under the Foreign Enlistment Act, which does not allow a man to entice or persuade another to enlist in the army. Mr. Henson, give me your version of the case."

I then told the whole truth, word for word, and did not dodge a single hair. I admitted that I had given John Alexander's wife provisions, and said " I would give them to any one, white or black, if I had them to give, and the individual needed them; but I did not suppose the man would turn my generosity against me in this base manner." I perceived that this was the only proof they had, and the man called it bribery on my part to get him to enlist.

Squire McLean said, "We all know Mr. Henson's character, that he is an honest, upright, Christian man. Now what is the character of his accuser? To-day is Saturday; I will defer my decision till Monday morning, and in the meantime inquiries can be made respecting the veracity of John Alexander."

How I should get released from the legal net that was spread over me I did not know, but I trusted in God; I knew He had delivered me many, many times before from the lions' den, and, like Daniel of olden times, I now put my faith in Him. In my heart I cried out, " O Lord, deliver me, but in prison, or under the free air of heaven, I will praise Thy great and holy name."

Still in the custody of the constable, I was allowed to go home on Saturday afternoon. A man called that night at my house and said to me, "There is a man loading his boat up the river, a bit; he comes from the same district where John Alexander lived before he prowled about Dresden. This Smith says Alexander is a thief, that he stole a lot of clothes from a line in a yard there, and other things, and a writ was taken out to apprehend him, but he ran away, and is now trying to send an innocent man to prison by telling a lot of lies, and he ought to be stopped."

As soon as this man left my house the constable gave me permission to call on Squire Terrace. This was Saturday evening. I gave him the drift of what the man had told me of Smith's knowledge of John Alexander. The squire said, "Go home and be quiet over Sunday, for Monday morning before the sun rises I will be at the river, and if I can find that Smith, and he testify as you have represented, I will have him in court on Monday morning by nine o'clock."

I remained quiet during Sunday, and my soul was full of joy and rejoicing, for this unlooked-for providence of God which I was sure would deliver me.

"Suppose he should not be found?" said one of my family. I answered, "But he will, I am certain." Though my fate hung upon a thread that might easily be cut, I anticipated no evil results.

Early on Monday morning Squire Terrace was at

the river's bank; he saw the boat half a mile off; he hailed it, and said, "Is there a man named Smith on that boat?" "I'm the man, sir." "Come ashore, I want to speak to you." This Smith then told the magistrate that he had worked with Alexander, and that "he was a mean, lying thief, and he could prove it." "Enough; I subpœna you to appear at the court this morning by nine o'clock to testify in this case," Squire Terrace answered.

The time came. It was understood at court that a witness would testify to the character of John Alexander, who was present in an exultant frame of mind. The witness was called. The attorney said, "You have worked with John Alexander; is he a trustworthy man? Has he a good, reliable character?" Smith said, "He is one of the greatest rogues out of prison." Alexander was about to interrupt him; but Smith looked him square in the face, and said, "You know if you stepped your foot where you used to work with me, you'd be hustled off to prison, where you ought to go if you got your deserts." Squire McDonald exclaimed, "What do you say? Is the man a rogue—has he no character?"

"He has none, sir; but was obliged to 'cut sticks,' as we say up in the country—that is, he gave 'leg bail' and ran away."

"Well," said Squire McDonald, "if John Alexander has no character, Mr. Henson has his acquittal." He was as much astounded at the appearance of the witness as my accuser was. It is needless to say that my friends and family re-

joiced with me at this signal deliverance. I sent
John Alexander word " that the world, or that part
of it where I lived, was too small for him and me ;
that if he crossed my path I was afraid I should be
tempted to shoot him." He was in terror, for he
knew he deserved shooting, or a severe castigation.
At last he sent by a couple of friends a humble
request for me to forgive him ; I told them he must
come to me personally and acknowledge his con-
temptible meanness in the presence of three of my
friends, whom I named. He came at an appointed
time, and on his knees he confessed his sin and
ingratitude to me for my kindness to his family, and
in the name of the Lord begged my forgiveness.

I said, " It was about the meanest thing you could
do to defame me in my absence, when my character
was one of the most precious things I had to cherish.
You ought to be hung, and I have been tempted to
dispatch you ; but I leave you in the hands of the
Lord ; vengeance belongeth to Him, and not to me.
I forgive you. Go and sin no more."

Not very long after, there was another peculiar
incident, connected with the civil war, which
threatened to give me some trouble. Many
in the States, both white and coloured, enlisted
merely to receive the bounty, and then they "jumped
the bounty," as it was termed—that is, they took
the money and did not go into the army. A friend
of mine, Alexander Pool, a coloured man of my
neighbourhood, told me " that his son and wife's
brother were talking about running away to join the
army, but he thought he ought to get a bounty for

them, and he wished I would take them to Detroit and advise them what to do." I replied, "I do not intend to subject myself to another trial on that score. I don't care whether they enlist or not; still, if they are going to the war, you ought to get some of their bounty, and it would enable you to pay for your land, but I can't enlist them."

He repeatedly asked my advice about the way to get to Detroit, and at length solicited me to accompany them there, and he offered to pay my expenses and for the time I lost. I said to the lads, "It is not my wish that you should enlist, but for your father's sake I will go to Detroit with you to protect you from the sharpers." We went, and they entered their names as Martin Pool and Basil Pool, and represented themselves as two brothers. I thought by this that probably their idea had been to run away, but the officer took possession of them and handed me a packet of money in an envelope directed to their father. I took from this package one hundred dollars and sent to the two lads. I took the remainder, eleven hundred dollars, to their father. He gave me four hundred for my expenses and trouble. The father had never seen so much money as he now had in his possession, but instead of using it for a good purpose he squandered it in dissipation. These lads went to the war, were in several battles, came back, and got their discharge. They demanded some of their bounty-money from their father. He pretended he had not received any. They said, "I must have kept it," and were very angry. They demanded it of me; but I indignantly told them "that they might go back to their father and ask him for it." They consulted a lawyer, who sent them to Squire McDonald, the same magistrate who conducted my case with John Alexander. He said, "I am surprised that Mr. Henson should have had anything to do with enlisting men, for he knows the law in such a case. I would advise you to make no stir in the matter, but to go with me to see him. Perhaps I can induce him to pay you something down, and then by instalments in the future to make up the difference." He called upon me with these lads, and said, "I am amazed to find that you have enlisted these young men and appropriated their bounty. I have called to suggest to you, Mr. Henson, to pay them something to-day, and then you can arrange to make up the balance at a more convenient time."

I replied, "Squire McDonald, I know nothing of what you refer to. I have not done what these men say." I turned to them and said, "I suppose you have your discharge-papers with you?" "Oh, yes," Basil Davis answered, eagerly, not suspecting in the least my purpose in wishing to see them. He pulled his out of his pocket. I turned to Squire McDonald and said, "You had better look after this man, he enlisted and was discharged under a false pretence; why didn't he use his right name, unless it was to enable him to run off and 'jump the bounty?' and now, because he could not succeed in escaping, but had to serve in the war, he must come back and vilify my name; you had better look after him."

The squire and his clients soon left me in peace. As their shadows were retreating I could not help laughing out loud and exclaiming, "Though there are more ways to kill a dog than feeding him on sweet cake, it will take cleverer lads to get the better of Father Henson than those who have just paid me a visit."   I, however, learned another lesson, and thought that in the future I had better let coloured volunteers gain wisdom and experience for themselves, without giving them either advice or personal assistance.

CHAPTER XXIX.

EARLY ASPIRATIONS CHECKED.

DESIRE TO LEARN TO SPELL NIPPED IN THE BUD.—SUPERSTITION. — INSURRECTION. — PREACHING AND ITS PENALTY. — NEGRO SONGS.

SHARP flashes of lightning come from black clouds, sprightly words of wit come from those who live in dark hovels, and bright gleams of intelligence come from children brought up in the most abject ignorance of books. It has often been a mystery to me how I gained a practical knowledge of figures, enough to sell all the produce of four farms during twenty-five years in the market at Washington, for I had to compute fractions and make great estimates, and yet I never studied arithmetic. I came in contact with many of the most intelligent gentlemen in Washington, for I used to take great pride in selecting the best butter for some of the best families, and was delighted to take it to their houses. They manifested a great interest in me, and when they conversed I listened attentively and remembered their phrases and sentences, and in this way I learned to speak more correctly than the majority of the slaves, or even the poor whites of the district. I never said "go dar," or "gib me," and other negro phrases, for I was anxious to imitate those whom I

respected as gentlemen.   I also gained a very good
practical knowledge of law from hearing clever
lawyers talk and explain their cases.   If I had been
a white boy and been blessed with the opportunities
to study law in my youth, I think I should have been
delighted with its study and practice.   The knowledge I "picked up" has enabled me in several instances to protect my own rights and those of my
people.

   I shall never forget my first attempts to learn to
spell.   I was about thirteen years of age, when I
nearly lost my life because I made an effort to gain
this kind of knowledge.   The schools for the white
children were generally four or five miles apart, and
a negro boy was accustomed to drive his master's
children in a waggon to school in the morning, and
to go for them in the afternoon.   A negro boy,
William, belonging to Lewis Bell, was a bright,
clever lad.   He learned to read and to spell by
hearing his master's boys talk about their lessons
while they were riding to and from school.   I was
so pleased to hear William read, that he told me if I
would buy a Webster's spelling-book in the store at
Washington he would soon teach me.   I had already
made some ink out of charcoal, and had cut a goose
quill so that it looked like my master's pen, and I
had begun to make scratches on odd bits of paper I
had picked up in the market.   I had noticed that
all the butter I sold was stamped with two letters,
"I. R.," and after awhile I learned that those
letters stood for my master, Isaac Riley, and I tried
and tried to imitate those marks, and they were
really the first letters I ever wrote.

It seemed to me if I took some of the apples that fell from the trees in the orchard and sold them I should be able to get the money for the spelling-book. I did this. Early the next morning I was about to harness the horse for my master; the horse was frisky and ran, and I ran to catch him, when my hat fell off and the book in it dropped on to the ground. After I had harnessed the horse my master exclaimed, " What's that ? " " A spelling-book." " Whose is it ? " " Mine." " Where did you get it ? " " Bought it, sir, when I went to market." " How much was it ? " " Eleven cents." " Where did you get the money ? " " I sold some apples out of our orchard." " Our orchard ! " he exclaimed, in a passion. " I'll teach you to get apples from our orchard for such a vile purpose, so you'll remember it. Give me that book." I stooped to pick it up, and as I saw his big cane coming down I dodged. " Pick up that book," he cried, using an awful oath. At last I was obliged to do it, when he beat me across the head and back till my eyes were swollen and I became unconscious. My poor mother found me in this state, and it was some time before I was able to be about my work again. When my master saw me after I recovered, he said, sneeringly, " So you want to be a fine gentleman ? Remember if you meddle with a book again I'll knock your brains out." The wonder to me is, why I have any brains left. I shall carry to my grave a scar my master made that day on my head. I did not open a book again till after I was forty-two years of age and out of the land of slavery. There was so much

N

excitement when it was understood by the masters that Lewis Bell's slave, William, was intending to teach their slaves, that William was sent to Georgia and sold, for the masters in our neighbourhood said, " We will not have our niggers spoiled by that rascal."

Many a time, when I was a young man, I have driven chickens and pigs into the woods and killed them in the night, and then taken them to the cabins of the feeble, sickly women, who had to work during the day under a hot sun, without having sufficient food to nourish them and their little babies.

I used to reason that the slaves were the property of their masters, and so were the pigs, and if accidentally the pigs got a sore throat, and I induced them to wander away, it was only taking a part of master's property, the pigs, to make the other part of his property, the women, more valuable. For the same reason, when I had a row to hoe between the rows of two women, I have often made them sit down and rest while I would hoe all three rows, and would give them a loud warning to get up if I perceived master was coming; in this way I have saved many women from beatings with the lash.

It is a singular fact that the law did not recognise it as stealing if a slave took any food from his master. If he stole a chicken from another plantation he could receive by law sixteen stripes at the public whipping-post, twenty stripes for a turkey, twenty-five or thirty for a pig, thirty-nine for a sheep, which was the highest. It is not surprising that slaves took all the food they could find, for their life was one of incessant toil, and they were scantily supplied with the poorest fare, which could not possibly give them strength. When removed from the debasing influences of slavery, the fugitives, as a general thing, had as keen perceptions of the sense of property as the white population. It has been an exceptional thing for a coloured man to steal after he reached Canada; and stealing is regarded by him as a disgraceful sin. He knows he can enjoy the proceeds of his own labour in the land of freedom, and all the fugitives in Canada can earn their own livelihood if they will exert themselves. At first they had to live on roots and herbs; but after a few years they began to own their own farms, to raise all kinds of grain and vegetables, and to cultivate a great variety of fruit-trees. All may now sit under their own vine and fig-tree. Some have asked me " if those who have been accustomed to a hot climate at the south, do not find the cold Canadian winters long and unpleasant?" I have only one reply to make to that query, "*that cool freedom is far better than hot oppression.*" It is easy to protect ourselves against the inclemency of the weather, but we could not ward off the blows of a cruel master, who was well aware that it was necessary to crush the manhood of the slave, to make him subservient to his master's selfish interests.

Superstition and ignorance are generally found in company together. Sixty years ago the whites in Maryland and Virginia were very ignorant. With the exception of the few who were educated at the north and the professional gentlemen, not one man

in 500 could write his name decently. There can
be seen at the present day many state-records and
documents in which the people have signed their
names by making a cross or a mark.   It is not
strange that among such people many were exceedingly superstitious. It is well known that the blacks
as a class were very superstitious, and believed in all
kinds of conjurations.

As a lad I was useful, very clever, and was often
called my master's "Man Friday," after Robinson
Crusoe's faithful servant. I soon perceived the weak
points in the character of my mistress, and that she
was very timid. She would sometimes complain if I
did not get as good prices for the provisions as she
desired, and I would hear of this through some of
the servants, or by putting my ear down to the door-
sill of the room where she was fretting to my master.
The next morning I would talk to a little ball I had
suspended to a delicate string which I held in my
fingers. A short distance off no one could see the
string, and as I talked to the ball it appeared to
bound up and then go down again without being
touched. "So Missis Riley thinks I didn't get
enough for her butter?" Up would come the ball.
"I got all it was worth?" Down the little ball
would go. It was astonishing what a reputation for
cleverness that ball obtained in my hands. "Why,
it knows everything," I once heard my mistress say.
If a dog howled, or a hen made an unusual noise,
there was some meaning attached to it, and an interpretation made. The negroes often imagined they
had frogs in their ankles or spiders in their throats,

and the spell had to be broken by some doctor who understood how to take advantage of this peculiar feature of the negro's mind.   Education soon clears away all this belief in witchcraft.

In many districts the blacks far outnumbered the whites.   Sometimes one planter had 400 negroes on an extensive plantation.   The year before Nat Turner's insurrection, for which he lost his life, there was an extensive organisation among the blacks who represented a district of fifty miles in extent, in the neighbourhood where I lived.   The plans were well-laid, every detail had been well-considered, even the time when the blow was to be struck had been appointed.

It was to be at eleven o'clock at night, when the moon was full at that time.   Certain slaves were to fire the barns and stables in all the different plantations comprised within the area, at the same hour. Then others were to be stationed at the houses, and as the masters rushed out to ascertain what the matter was, the slaves were to kill them and then kill the entire families, and burn up their houses. " Not one white shall be left to tell the tale!" exclaimed an excited slave.   I could not agree with the leaders, and yet I felt that the evils of slavery could not be exaggerated, and that we had a right to our freedom.   Little by little the light came to my soul, till I was convinced that it was not a feasible or Christian plan of procedure ; so I began to raise doubts and queries, to discuss the subject, and finally, I had the moral courage to speak my mind plainly. I said, " Suppose we should kill one thousand of the white population, we should surely lose our own lives, and make the chains of those in bondage heavier and more securely riveted. No, let us suffer in God's name, and wait His time for Ethiopia to stretch forth her hands and be free." At last I prevailed on them to abandon the project. It is certain that the slaves had provocation enough to rise and take the places of their masters. I saw at one time, a faithful fellow-workman receive 500 lashes on his bare back, simply because, when he was a little tardy, he resisted being beaten by a cane over the head. He was nearly dead when he was given into my care for me to look after his condition.

After I began to preach, I just escaped receiving thirty-nine lashes at the public whipping-post in Alexandria, near Washington, simply for asking the Mayor to give me permission to comply with a request to preach there. He indignantly ordered me to be taken to prison on the Saturday, and to receive the whipping on the Monday or to pay a fine of 25 dollars. I had no money, and I prayed to God to show me what to do. At last I found some one to send to my master's young brother. He came to see me in jail, and by giving him my watch, worth 45 dollars, he paid the fine and I was released. Before we left the city, however, the blacks collected around me, and the Lord opened my mouth, and I had the moral courage to give them such a sermon as they had not heard for a long time. As soon as I had finished my sermon, my young master, who was ready with his waggon, hurried me into it, and we rode out of the city in great haste, for, as he told me, the law would not allow me to preach openly to a number of slaves in that district.

Under very different influences, I was talking or preaching to a very large audience of intelligent white ladies and gentlemen in Tremont Temple, Boston, Mass., after I had escaped from slavery. I had nearly finished my discourse, when, wrought up to the highest pitch of excitement, I exclaimed, " I wish I had the entire control of the southern slave-holders for twenty-four hours !" A man at the extreme end of that large hall jumped up, and said, excitedly, " Mr. Chairman, may I ask the speaker one question ?" The gentleman who presided, fear-ing that the man intended to raise a row, said, mildly, " Mr. Henson has the platform, and no one must interrupt him without his permission." I said, " The gentleman at the back of the house may ask me the question." He rose, and, in an excited manner, rather sneeringly asked, " And pray, what would you do with them ?"

There was a breathless silence, and all my friends were anxious, not knowing how much I might be agitated by my past memories of the cruelty of slave-holders, and that I had cause for revengeful feelings, if I did not manifest them. I said, in as loud and deep a voice as I could command, " First, I would have them all thoroughly converted to God; and secondly, I would send them immediately to heaven, before they had one minute's time to backslide." I then sat down, and there was such an uproar of cheers and hurrahs as I had never heard at any meeting.

I may as well close this chapter by giving a

sample of the songs the slaves sing when the family is about to separate because some of the members have been sold to new masters. Sometimes they sing these plaintive melodies, clanking their chains to keep time with their voices.

> When I was down in Egypt's land,
> Close by the river,
> I heard one tell of the promised land,
> Down by the river side.

> *Chorus.* We'll end this strife,
>   Down by the river,
> We'll end this strife,
>   Down by the river side.

> I never shall forget this day,
> Down by the river,
> When Jesus washed my sins away,
> Down by the river side.
>   *Chorus.*

> 'Twas just before the break of day,
> Down by the river,
> When Jesus washed my sins away,
> Down by the river side.
>   *Chorus.*

> Cheer up, cheer up, we're gaining ground
> Down by the river.
> Old Satan's kingdom we'll pull down,
> Down by the river side.
>   *Chorus.*

> Shout, dear children, for you are free,
> Down by the river,
> Christ has brought to you, liberty,
> Down by the river side.
>   *Chorus.*

CHAPTER XXX.

MY FAMILY.

A NEW LIGHT IN MY DESOLATE HOME.—MY CHILDREN.—MY THIRD VISIT TO ENGLAND.—MR. HUGHES.

MY heart and home were desolate after I lost the wife who had been my faithful companion in slavery, and had escaped with me to Canada. For four years it seemed to me her place could not be filled. I kept company with no one; I never walked out with any woman, and I thought it would be so to the end; but I was so lonely, so utterly miserable, that at last I decided that I would try to find another companion. I had travelled extensively, and had made many acquaintances, but I knew of but one woman whom I cared to have for a wife. She was a widow, an estimable woman, one who had been a faithful teacher in the Sunday school, and quite a mother in the church to which she belonged. She had been brought up by a Quaker lady in Baltimore, and had received a good education in the ordinary branches. Her mother had been a slave, but was such a superior laundress, that she earned enough to buy her freedom of her mistress, and then she earned enough to buy her husband's freedom.   One of her daughters has lived for many years with a family, and she has travelled with them around the world.

I went to Boston and called upon the pleasant widow several times before I could summon the courage to ask her if she would be my wife.   It was about two years before we were married in Boston by our bishop, who was holding a series of meetings at the time in the city.   She has made me an excellent wife, and my cup has indeed run over with God's mercies.   She had one son and two daughters. I have now seven living children.   My eldest son, Tom, went to California, and I think was killed in the civil war, for I have not heard from him since he enlisted.   Isaac, my second son, was a clever and godly lad.   He was educated in a school in London for many years through the kindness of my London friends.   He married, was ordained as a Wesleyan minister, and preached for about fifteen years.   He died when only thirty-seven, and was universally beloved.   My third son, Josiah, was very anxious to learn the shoemaker's trade, but I persuaded him to help me on my farm.   At twenty-two he married a very capable young woman, and then he said, "I am determined now to have my own way, father ; I've tried to stick to the farm, but I can't do so any longer ; I know I can make my way."   He left Canada, and went to Jackson, Michigan, where there was a great prejudice against employing coloured young men in the shoe-business.   He found an English boot and shoe-maker there who agreed to teach him.   He was bound to him for two years.

His young wife was a good washer and ironer, and
she went out to work by the day, and obtained excellent wages, and the young people were very
happy. At the end of the two years his master
said to me, " Young Josiah Henson is a clever fellow.
He can make as good a boot as his master." My
son then went to Adrian, where there was an anti-
slavery college. He bought a couple of lots of
ground in time. He worked at his trade during the
winter, and in the spring went out to do lathing,
plastering, and hanging paper in the houses of some
of the best people. He was very fond of horticul-
ture, and has cultivated a great variety of fruit
trees. He has continued to do well, and now has
property worth several thousand dollars. My fourth
son, Peter, is a farmer, looks after my farm, and
stays with me.

My four daughters are married; all of them can
read and write very well, and one of them has been
educated for two years in Oberlin. There has been
a great change in the condition of the coloured
people since I first went to Canada. Then, there
was not a Bible or a hymn-book for a coloured individual to use for several hundred miles; and none of
us could have read the Bible if we had possessed
one; but now there are in every cabin the elements
of education. When it was known I had preached
at the South, I had urgent requests to labour in this
way in Canada, and as a Methodist episcopal elder I
have had a district of three hundred miles, over
which I have travelled, held meetings, attended
conferences, have established churches, and been

interested in every movement that has been started for the improvement of our people.

We have had great assistance from the late Rev. Mr. Hughes, the Secretary of the Colonial and Continental Missionary Church Society in Canada (who died April 11th, 1876). For sixteen or seventeen years he worked most zealously as a missionary in Canada; he was always my devoted friend; he knew all my troubles with regard to the school, that my finances had been crippled by my mortgaging my property to pay the expenses of that lawsuit during seven years, and he proposed that I should again visit London in my old age, and he assured me that my old friends would rally to my assistance. It was a sad day to me when, only three months before I left Canada, I was summoned to his dying bedside. His last moments were peaceful, and his faith to the last was triumphant. He died as he had lived, a genuine Christian. In the last annual report of the Colonial and Continental Church Society, which has reached me since I came to London, he has kindly referred to my mission in London as follows: "Josiah Henson (Mrs. Stowe's ' Uncle Tom '), who, I think you are aware, resides near Dresden, proposes starting in a week or two for England. His principal object will be to try to raise money to clear off a heavy mortgage he had to give on his farm in order to meet the costs of the long lawsuit over the Dawn Institute property, and which but for him would have been entirely lost. Mr. Henson bore the whole expense of that suit, and when the case was settled it was found that the trustees, appointed by the Court of Chancery, had no power to refund him out of the estate. The proceeds of the sale of the Dawn property, nearly 30,000 dollars, constitute the greater part of the endowment of the Wilberforce Educational Institute. You will be pleased to learn that this institute is now in active operation, and if only wisely managed in the future will be a great blessing, in an educational point of view, to the coloured people of Canada. A voyage to England is no light undertaking for a man of Henson's extreme age, he being now eighty-seven. Though he is not by any means the man he was when in England twenty-five years ago, yet he still possesses extraordinary energy both of body and mind, and knowing, as I do, his circumstances, and the hardship of his case, I sincerely hope he may be successful."

It may be well to add a few of many testimonials I received, when it was known I intended to visit England :—

" We, the undersigned, beg to certify that we have known the Reverend Josiah Henson for a number of years ; that he has resided, as we believe, in the County of Kent, Ontario, for the last forty-five years ; that he has ever borne the highest character in this community, and is worthy of the confidence of the public.—Wm. Bryant Wells, Judge C. C. Co. Kent, Ontario ; John Mercer, Sheriff, Kent ; Wm. Douglas, Clerk of the Peace, Kent ; H. Smythe, Mayor, Town of Chatham ; Francis W. Sandys, A.M., Archdeacon of Kent, Ontario.—Chatham, 25th April, 1876."

"Memorial Church Rectory, London, Ontario, May 16, 1876.—To the Secretaries of the Colonial and Continental Church Society.—Dear Sirs,—In the last report to the Society, our lamented friend Mr. Hughes speaks of a proposed visit to England of the Rev. Josiah Henson (Mrs. Stowe's 'Uncle Tom') for the purpose of raising funds to clear off a mortgage which Mr. Henson had to give on his farm in order to meet the costs of a lawsuit over the Dawn Institute. The object of this note is to introduce him to you, hoping that you may be able to further his cause in England. He was well known to the friends of the coloured race twenty years ago, but the changes make it essential that he should have some who can recommend him in his present effort. You are already acquainted with the work of the Wilberforce Institute, which has been sustained at great personal expense by Mr. Henson. His experience as a slave, and as a preacher among the fugitives in Canada, makes his story extremely interesting. Mrs. Stowe, in her 'Key to Uncle Tom's Cabin,' gives a sketch of his life to confirm the character she has painted. On the authority of Mr. Hughes, who knew Mr. Henson for many years, and thought most highly of his work and character, I beg to introduce to you one who has been a great blessing to his coloured brethren in Canada. If you can give him any letters, or further his cause in any way, it will assist the movement with which the Colonial and Continental Church Society has been connected for many years.—Yours very sincerely, W. Harrison Tilley, Clerical Secretary to Corresponding Committee, Colonial and Continental Church Society."

"Dresden, Ontario, Canada, March 10, 1876.—Mr. Josiah Henson being about to proceed to England, has requested me to give him a letter testimonial. Mr. Henson is so highly respected throughout Western Canada, and also so well known to many influential persons, both in the United States and in England, that he scarcely needs anything of the kind from any individual. I have known Mr. Henson for more than sixteen years, and have great pleasure in bearing my testimony to his sterling Christian character. Mr. Henson's life has been an unusually active and eventful one. For many years he was a slave, and was most cruelly treated; and since his escape to Canada, now more than forty years ago, he has occupied a foremost place in all movements for the advancement of his people. Through his efforts for their good he has, unfortunately, suffered considerable pecuniary loss, and has been compelled in consequence to mortgage his farm. It is with the view of lifting this incumbrance that he has, in his extreme old age, resolved, in response to a cordial invitation given him, to visit England. I heartily commend him and his cause to the British public, and hope that he may have, in every respect, a 'prosperous journey by the will of God.'—Thos. Hughes, Missionary of the Church of England, Dresden."

CHAPTER XXXI.

MY THIRD AND LAST VISIT TO LONDON.

MEETING OLD FRIENDS AND MAKING NEW ONES.—"CHRISTIAN AGE."—PROF. FOWLER'S DESCRIPTION.—MY MISSION ACCOMPLISHED.

AFTER the lapse of twenty-five years I was delighted to be in London again. Many of the friends whom I had known during my former visit have passed away. I found that Samuel Morley, Esq., and George Sturge, Esq., remembered me most kindly, and that they were disposed to be my staunch, steadfast friends; they have been genuine friends to me during all these long years that have passed, and I hope to greet them when we have all passed over the River Jordan. They at once promised to aid me in removing the weight that was pressing down my spirits and embarrassing my declining years when I could not labour as formerly. They started a fund, and generously headed it, not only with their influential names, but each gave £50 towards it. May God bless them for their generosity, and for their abiding friendship to me. Sir Thomas Fowell Buxton, Bart., and R. C. L. Bevan, added £25 each to the fund, and many belonging to the Society of Friends added their subscriptions. I should like to record that I have always received the most generous treatment, both in America and England, from the members of the Friends' Society, and specially from George Sturge, Esq., who has interested himself to the extent of assuring me he would send me back to my Canadian home with a light heart. I am certain my heart will be *heavy with gratitude*, for it will be full of that emotion, and I shall pray to my dying day for blessings to rest upon one who has afforded me so much relief.

Among the new friends I have made are Professor and Mrs. Fowler, formerly of New York, now residing in London, and I have always felt at home in their pleasant office.

Professor Fowler, with his remarkable skill, gave me an analysis of my character from my head. I told him " I should have supposed my old master had beaten out all my brains," but he humorously remarked " that perhaps my skull was so thick, the blows did not penetrate."

The description he gave of me was published, with my portrait, in the *Christian Age*, a weekly paper, and notwithstanding there were 80,000 copies of this number circulated, a third edition had to be printed to meet the demand. I am sure Professor Fowler's description will be of interest, and therefore give it insertion here.

" The *organisation* of 'Uncle Tom' is as remarkable as his life and labours have been. His father was six feet in height, and was a very powerful, muscular man. He had a strong sense of justice and virtue, and an unflinching will. His son, Uncle Tom, is five feet seven inches in height.

o

"From his father he inherited a very strong osseous, muscular system, and a powerful constitution, as his physiology indicates and his most laborious life has proved. He has a large brain, twenty-three inches in circumference, with a predominance of brain in the superior coronal region, indicating great mental vigour, compass of mind, and availability of talent. His head is narrow, long, and high. The strength of his *social* nature centres in love to his wife and children, especially the latter, which he has proved to be intense, by his carrying two of his children on his back 600 miles, travelling on foot during the night, while fleeing from slavery and seeking his freedom on British soil in Canada. His head is very high in the crown and above the ears. No white man has a greater sense of liberty, love of freedom, manliness of feeling, and independence of mind, joined to a degree of firmness, perseverance, and determination of mind, not exceeded by a Cromwell or a Wellington, than Uncle Tom. His sense of *moral* obligations and love of truth are very strong.

"He is scrupulously honest, and his mind is as transparent as daylight. He is not inclined to double dealing, deception, and hypocrisy, undue selfishness or greed in his disposition, but he is cautious, looks ahead, and prepares for the future.

"He has by organisation, as well as by grace, a strong feeling of devotion, worship, and sense of dependence. As a Christian, some of his strongest religious feelings are his love of prayer and thankfulness, and his disposition to seek aid and consolation from a higher source than man in the hour of trouble. The exercise of his *veneration* was his com-

fort when a slave, and it has been a comfort to him
through all the vicissitudes of life. *Benevolence* is
also very large; he is full of the missionary
element, delights to do good, and many years
of his life have been spent in labours of love. He
is liable to forget his own interests when he can
make himself useful to others. In his mind, 'faith
without works is dead.' He does not expect an
answer to his prayers without he makes an effort in
the right direction. He is active, industrious, and
delights to be occupied; is always busy in one way
or another; and is not afraid of hard work if necessary. His mind works slowly but quite safely.
When he has an object he holds on to it till his end
is accomplished. He is one of the real plodding
kind. He has not the qualities to render him showy
and imaginative, but he has good powers of imitation,
and can easily adapt himself to a change of situation
and circumstances. He has a vast amount of dry
humour, and is very direct, practical, natural, and
truthful in his style of talking. His intellectual
faculties are of the most practical and common-sense
kind.

"He has superior powers to draw correct conclusions
and inferences, as he understands them. He deals
mostly in facts, conditions, qualities, and bearings
of things, and turns all his knowledge into useful
channels. He has a remarkable gift for observing
everything that is transpiring around him; has a
superior memory of persons he sees, facts he hears,
of places, events, and anecdotes; and his mind is
like a great storehouse, in which he has collected a
vast amount of interesting incidents. He has a good

capacity to arrange, systematise, organise, and plan, with reference to definite results.

"He is a great lover of simple truths; acts and speaks just as he feels, and thinks instinctively; cannot assume a character and appear differently from what he really feels, and has a thorough abhorrence of hypocrisy or falsehood. He has great courage in times of danger, also great presence of mind and great self-control in the midst of excitement and opposition.

"He is not revengeful, but has any amount of contemptuous feeling towards those who act meanly. He is more direct in his style of talking than copious or wordy; yet, having but little restraint from *secretiveness*, and so much varied knowledge and experience, he finds it easy to talk when he has attentive listeners.

"Though in his eighty-eighth year, he appears to be at least fifteen years younger, for he is firm in step, erect in form, disposed to wait on himself, and prefers to walk rather than ride; is positive in his manner of speaking, social in his disposition, emotional in his feelings, tender in his sympathies, distinct in his intellectual operations, humorous in his conversation, and apt in his illustrations. While many at fifty years of age consider that there is no opportunity left for them to improve their condition, Uncle Tom, at eighty-eight, is buoyant, elastic, and still anxious to make improvements.

"I have been much gratified in making the acquaintance of 'Uncle Tom,' and hope the friends of the coloured race in England will send him back to

Canada with sufficient means to enable him to live in comfort the remainder of his days."

Another of my new friends is Mr. John Lobb (the managing editor of the *Christian Age*). He has an extensive acquaintance with most of the evangelical ministers in London. He has arranged all my engagements, assisted me in addressing, at their request, very large audiences in public buildings, chapels, and places of worship. Indeed, he has on every public occasion rendered me material assistance as my *Chairman*. Under such obligations, I felt it to be a pleasant duty to make some acceptable acknowledgment, which I trust it will prove to be. I have therefore assigned the sole copyright of this work to Mr. JOHN LOBB.

On my visit to London in 1851, I had made acquaintance with the family of Mr. Thomas Church, author of " Gospel Victories," and was glad to renew our friendship and love in 1876. I thank him for so ably assisting in my correspondence while in London.

I cannot omit to acknowledge my obligations to Dr. Macaulay, of the Religious Tract Society, and the able editor of a widely prized monthly, called the *Sunday at Home*. To other remembrances of kindness, I feel thankful for his excellent article in the October part for 1876, headed "Uncle Tom," and his confirmatory observations in favour of my history, and the object of my present visit to London.

Invitations have come from all parts of England, Ireland, and Scotland, for me to speak to the people, but my strength was not sufficient to undertake all. I copy from the *Christian Age*, the following

"SUMMARY OF 'UNCLE TOM'S' PUBLIC SERVICES.

IN *August*, 1876, on Sunday, at Victoria Park Tabernacle, to a congregation exceeding 2,000 persons.

At Wood Green, on Thursday, in the "Tent" erected for evangelistic services by T. B. Smithies, Esq., editor of the "British Workman." In the unavoidable absence of Baroness Coutts, she kindly deputed Rev. Mr. Sinclair to take her carriage and place it at "Uncle Tom's" service at the close of the proceedings.

In September, 1876, again at *Wood Green*, in the Wesleyan chapel, which accommodated over 1,000 persons.

Little Wild Street Baptist Chapel, Drury Lane.—Crowded beyond the capacity of the place.

Epsom.—This neighbourhood has been rarely moved with an excitement like that which followed "Uncle Tom's" visit here.

Brixton.—On Friday, at the Congregational Church, to a large and appreciative audience.

Mildmay Park.—On Sunday, in this large and beautiful Conference Hall; although it seats 2,500 persons, the building was crowded in every part, and hundreds failed to gain admission.

Stoke Newington.—On Sunday evening, in the Congregational Church, Walford Road.

Wallington.—On Wednesday the place of meeting was thronged. Rev. Dr. Whittemore, and Rev. J. Williams, of the vicarage, taking part in the proceedings.

New North Road Congregational Church, though capacious, was overcrowded on Thursday; and a second meeting in the large schoolroom was conducted at the same time, "Uncle Tom," after the chapel address, adjourning to supplement the other meeting, to the intense delight of all.

Milton Road Congregational Church, in Stoke Newington, was also crowded in every part by a large company.

Mayfield Terrace Wesleyan Chapel on Sunday was, though large and commodious, filled to overflowing.

Mile End.—On Sunday, the great tent belonging to F. N. Charrington, Esq., was filled, "Uncle Tom" also delivering a lecture on the Monday evening.

The South Coast.—During the week "Uncle Tom" addressed large audiences in Portsmouth, Southampton, and in the Town Hall at Ryde, Isle of Wight.

Her Majesty's Ship "Victory."—"Uncle Tom" visited this famous vessel, which bore Nelson's flag, and on the deck of which he received his death-wound in the moment of triumph over the combined fleets of France and Spain, off Cape Trafalgar. By command, the whole of the ship's officers and crew were collected to receive an address from "Uncle Tom." To each of the company a copy was presented of the *Christian Age*, containing "Uncle Tom's" portrait.

Peniel Tabernacle, Haverstock Road.—This Baptist chapel was thronged on Sunday to hear a sermon from "Uncle Tom."

Victoria Park Tabernacle.—On Sunday evening this capacious iron church, the largest in England, accommodating 2,000 persons, was again crammed in every part.

South Hackney.—On Wednesday, by invite of Lady Seymour, at Wilton House "Uncle Tom" delivered an effective address to the members of that lady's classes. All present were deeply affected, and three resolved to give their hearts to God. "Uncle Tom" will never forget this meeting.

Winchmore Hill Congregational Church.—An interesting meeting thronged this place of worship, and "Uncle Tom" spoke with good effect.

In October, 1876.—On Sunday, at Putney Congregational Church, Oxford Road, "Uncle Tom" delivered telling addresses in the afternoon and evening, under a gracious influence.

Wesley's Chapel, City Road.—On Tuesday, by the kind invite of J. W. Gabriel, Esq. (brother of the Alderman, and late Lord Mayor), Rev. J. Henson and Mr. Lobb met a select party of friends to tea, and afterwards repaired to this sanctuary, so sacredly memorable to Methodists everywhere, for its history and associations. It was properly felt by the brethren, Henson and Lobb, to be the most acceptable incident of their lives, and a powerful reminder of the sainted Wesley's ministry, from the very pulpit, which they occupied for about two hours! The occasion was Radnor Street school anniversary, and Rev. J. Henson announced to preach on its behalf. City Road Chapel was full, and overflowing by hundreds.

Bromley, Kent.—The residence of M. H. Hodder, Esq., was visited by "Uncle Tom," and an address given at this, the third anniversary of an evangelical mission, promoted in this locality by Mr. Hodder and his estimable wife, G. Williams, Esq., of the Young Men's Christian Association, taking part in the proceedings.

Twickenham.—"Uncle Tom's" meeting was held here in the Old Chapel Royal, and Rev. F. J. C. Moran, B.D., Secretary of the "Colonial and Continental Church Society," which is under the patronage of Her Majesty the Queen, took part in the proceedings, which were successful.

Haverstock Road.—Peniel Tabernacle had a second visit from "Uncle Tom," with much success.

Hinde Street Chapel, Manchester Square, was the scene of a successful meeting.

Weigh House Chapel, London Bridge.—This was the famous centre of influence under Rev. Thomas Binney's ministry, and is succeeded by a worthy successor, Rev. W. Braden. "Uncle Tom" attended a deeply interesting service here.

Whitfield Tabernacle, Tottenham Court Road.—An interesting gathering.

Sloane Street Chapel, Chelsea, a celebrated Wesleyan chapel, was the scene of a delightful "Uncle Tom" meeting.

Messrs. Hitchcock and Williams', St. Paul's Churchyard.—
"Uncle Tom" gave an address here to the employees, George
Williams, Esq., founder of "The Young Men's Christian Association," presiding. Mr. John Lobb, on introducing "Uncle Tom,"
said, "Here is the hero of Mrs. Harriet Beecher Stowe's "Uncle
Tom's Cabin;" the "Uncle Tom" who rescued *Eva* from a
watery grave; the "Uncle Tom" who accompanied *George Harris*
to Mrs. H. B. Stowe's residence, whose united history furnished
her with such interesting records as appear in "Uncle Tom's
Cabin," of world-wide fame; the "Uncle Tom," too, so maimed
for life by *Legree,* but whose real name is Bryce Litton, as recorded in Mr. Henson's "Life," and confirmed in pages 34 to 57 of
Mrs. Stowe's Key to "Uncle Tom's Cabin."

Victoria Park Tabernacle.—Over 2,000 persons were present,
when a handsomely composed testimonial, duly framed, was presented to 'UNCLE TOM.'"

FINIS.

APPENDIX A.

A SKETCH OF MRS. H. BEECHER STOWE.

ALTHOUGH this esteemed lady, of a noble family, enjoys a
world-wide fame, there may probably be many to whom
the succeeding lines, descriptive of her character and history,
will be of interest. Her father was Lyman Beecher, D.D., born in
1771, and, until of mature age, he was brought up to the trade of
his father, a blacksmith. After leaving it for a course of study at
Yale College, New Haven, he entered upon the work of the ministry.
For some time Dr. Lyman Beecher was pastor of a church at Lich-
field, and here Harriet Beecher was born, A.D. 1812. Ultimately
he removed to Boston; and in 1832 quitted it for Lane, in Cincinnati. Here Lyman Beecher took charge of the seminary, and sought
to establish collegiate studies in connection with self-supporting
labour. In this enterprise Professor Calvin Stowe took part, and
for a time their work prospered. The slavery then existing in the
United States led to its overthrow. The year 1830 had witnessed
the French revolution. An agitation had sprung up in England

against Colonial Slavery. American judicial courts had imprisoned and fined many who had spoken against slavery. All these historic facts called the attention of philanthropists in the United States to the evils and crime of slavery; Dr. Beecher's seminary could not resist the rising discussion of that crowned iniquity! The mob threatened, and Kentucky slaveholders went over to urge it on to violence. To save the property, the trustees interfered, and calmed the mob by the assurance that slavery should not further be discussed in the seminary. Another rebellion came from within, for the students *refused* to obey the order of the trustees, and left the seminary in a body. For years Beecher and Stowe sought in vain to restore the prosperity of that seminary. In 1850 they returned to the Eastern States—Stowe to the Professor's chair of Biblical literature in Andover Theological Seminary, and Lyman Beecher to the work of the ministry in Cincinnati.

Harriet Beecher spent eighteen years in this Lane Seminary; having previously assisted her sister Catharine, in the conduct of a training school for female teachers. Cincinnati is a city situated on the northern bank of the Ohio; and upon the high hill, whose point, crowned with an observatory, overhanging the city on the west, was Lane Seminary. The village nearest to it was called the Walnut Hills and one of the prettiest in the environs. It was here, therefore, that Harriet Beecher lived, and helped her sister in teaching, until her marriage, at the age of twenty-five, with Professor Calvin E. Stowe, of the Seminary, over which her father then was president. But few of Mrs. H. Beecher-Stowe's numerous offspring have survived. Mrs. Stowe says :—

"Charlie, the most beautiful of my children, and the most beloved, lies buried near my Cincinnati residence. It was at his dying bed and at his grave that I learnt what a poor slave-mother may feel when her child is torn from her. In the depths of my sorrow, which seemed to me immeasurable, it was my only prayer to God that such anguish might not be suffered in vain.

"There were circumstances connected with this child's death of such peculiar bitterness—of what might seem almost cruel suffering —that I felt I could never be consoled for it, unless it should appear that the crushing of my own heart might enable me to work out some great good to others.

"His death took place during the cholera-summer, when in a circle of five miles around me, 9,000 were buried—a mortality which I have never heard exceeded anywhere.

"My husband, in feeble health, was obliged to be absent the whole time, and I had sole charge of a family of fifteen persons. He did not return to me, because I would not permit it; for in many instances where parents had returned from a distance to their families, and to the infected atmosphere, the result had been sudden death, and the physicians warned me that if he returned, it would only be to die. My poor Charlie died for want of timely medical aid; for in the universal confusion and despair that prevailed, it was often impossible to obtain assistance till it was too late."

Between 1835 and 1847, Cincinnati became the prominent battle-ground of freedom and slavery. It will now be clear to the reader how painfully familiar Mrs. H. B. Stowe became with the horrors of slavery. The road which ran through Walnut Hills, only a few feet from Mrs. Stowe's door, was ultimately a favourite route of "The Underground Railway," so called, and so familiar in the pages of "Uncle Tom's Cabin." The "railway" consisted of a noble line of Quakers and other anti-slavery friends, who lived at intervals, say, of fifteen or twenty miles, between the Ohio River and the Northern Lakes. These friends had combined to help fugitive slaves forward in their escape to Canada. A fugitive would be taken at night, on horseback or in a covered waggon, from station to station, as described, until *he* stood on a free soil, and found the British banner floating o'er his head. Or,

> "Thus when *her* form flits wildly by,
>   With bloodless cheek and fearless eye,
>   Resolved to free her child or die,
>   We still our very breath—
>   Till, safely on the farther shore
>   She stands, the desperate journey o'er
>   So fraught with life and death."

Referring once more to the "Underground Railway," we may remind our readers that the first station north of Cincinnati was a few miles up Mill Creek, at the house of the pious and lion-hearted Vanzant, otherwise called Van Trompe in "Uncle Tom's Cabin." Such being the roadway, Mrs. Stowe would inevitably be roused, and frequently, by the rapid rattle of the covered waggons, and the noisy galloping of the horses ridden by the constables and slave-catchers, who would be in hot pursuit as they madly passed her door. Vanzant (the "Honest John," as he was called) was always ready to turn out with his team, and the hunters were rarely clever enough to come up with him. He has long since filled a martyr's grave. Mrs. Stowe, therefore, during her long residence on the frontier of the slave states, by several visits to them, would natu-rally become familiar in observations of them, and furnish herself with ample material for her masterpiece on slavery. We cannot refuse one of Mrs. Stowe's sketches in 1840. "The slave-catchers, backed by the riff-raff of the population, and urged on by certain politicians and merchants, attacked the quarters in which the negroes reside. Some of the houses were battered down by cannon. For several days the city was abandoned to violence and crime. The negro-quarters were pillaged and sacked. Negroes attempting to defend their property were killed, and their bodies thrown into the streets. Women cruelly injured by ruffians, some afterwards dying of their injuries. Houses were burnt, and men, women, and children were betrayed in the confusion, and hurried into slavery. From the brow of the hill on which I lived, I could hear the cries of the victims, the shouts of the mob, the reports of guns and cannon, and could see the flames of the conflagration. To more than one of the trembling fugitives I have given shelter, and wept bitter tears with them. After the fury of the mob was spent, many of the coloured people gathered together the little left them of worldly goods and started for Canada. Hundreds passed in front of my house. Some of them were in little waggons. Some trudging along on foot after their household stuff. Some leading their children by the hand. And there were even mothers who walked on suckling their infants, and weeping for the dead, or kidnapped husbands they had left behind." Before concluding this sketch we would observe that, by the verdict of England's people, "'Uncle Tom's Cabin' takes its place as a standard work amongst the beauties of English literature." As Earl Carlisle said : "Its genius, pathos, and humour, commend themselves." As the Rev. James Sherman said : "It is as irresistibly attractive to the learned and unlearned as Bunyan's Pilgrim's Progress." It has been translated in France, Holland, Germany, Italy, Sweden, Russia, and Spain. The supreme joy, however, to Mrs. Stowe must have been that Providence has prolonged her valuable life to witness the consummation of her prayers and toils—the *abolition* of slavery ! A more recent pleasure is, that the hero of her "Cabin," "Uncle Tom," has paid his third visit to England, even in his eighty-eighth year ! Rev. J. Henson (who supplied the principal facts of his life to Mrs. Stowe, and upon which she built her inimitable work of "Uncle Tom ") has been received in town and country with great interest, and by many thousands of people. Among other objects of interest in his travels, he has addressed the officers and crew of Lord Nelson's line-of-battle ship—the old "Trafalgar."

May the closing years of Mrs. Stowe and Josiah Henson be happy and triumphant ! May the fruits of their spiritual life-work swell the "multitude of the redeemed ! " The night is short, and the morning will soon dawn !

APPENDIX B.

"A LOST CONTINENT."

SLAVERY AND THE SLAVE-TRADE IN AFRICA AS IT NOW IS.

[By the kind permission of the author, Joseph Cooper, Esq., we earnestly enlist the attention and sympathy of our readers to the following extracts which we have taken from his mournfully interesting work, entitled, "A Lost Continent," published by Messrs. Longmans, Green, and Co.]

"When the events of the present age pass into history, probably no greater anomaly will be observed than the state of the vast continent of Africa during this part of the present century. The slave-trade at the present time extends over the greater part of the northern, southern, and central regions, and covers an area nearly *equal* to that of the whole of Europe."

"Notwithstanding all that has been done, the African slave-trade as a whole, is, at this moment, probably as great as it has been at any previous time."

"The slave-trade has now existed more than three centuries, and within that period, according to a careful French writer, more than fifty millions of slaves have been taken from Africa."

"The traffic mostly now carried on by the overland routes eastward has enormously increased. The principal countries on behalf of which the present African slave-trade is carried on are Turkey, Egypt, Persia, Tunis, Morocco, and Madagascar. On them the responsibility for the present state of Africa now mainly rests."

"Sir Bartle Frere, in the Blue Book presented to the Houses of Parliament in 1873, states that, 'The correspondence of the Central African Vicariate Apostolic extends over countries roughly estimated at having a population of 80,000,000 of negroes, between the Red and Arabian Seas on the east, and the Atlantic on the west; and the annual drain consequent on slavery is estimated by the Superior of the Mission at 1,000,000.' Dr. Livingstone calculated that not more than one slave in five arrived at his destination, and on some routes not one in nine. This does not include the loss of life caused by the torture of boys for the markets of Egypt and Turkey, under which two out of every three perish."

"In all the expeditions it should be borne in mind that the cause of the natives is never heard. We only hear the statements of the Europeans who enter into these engagements, and they go so equipped and armed that, it has been forcibly remarked, their lives are insured. When any great amount of slaughter has been committed the aggressors congratulate one another on their bravery and gallant bearing, and the world applauds."

"At the present moment England, France, and America may, in a certain sense, be said to patronise slavery in the East. Their Consuls in those countries appoint agents in the principal towns and centres who are supporters of slavery and owners of slaves. Over the roofs of their houses wave the flags of Christian nations, and under them are the slaves of these Consular Agents."

"The following remarks are taken from a very important paper written in Egypt, by Sir Bartle Frere, on his route to Zanzibar:— 'It can hardly escape so enlightened a ruler as His Highness that slavery is in itself a canker which must eat into the vitals of a country like Egypt, whose prosperity depends in so large a degree on the industry of the agricultural class. . . . His Highness expressed a hope that the stoppage of the supply of slaves from the interior would ultimately tend towards a gradual diminution and final extinction of slavery in Egypt. *I feel that all experience is against this expectation. Whilst the demand continues I believe it to be practically impossible to cut off the supply.* This is especially the case where the sources of supply are so many and spread over so large an area that ages would hardly suffice to reach them all by separate measures of repression. But if the demand is extinguished the object is at once effected and the trade must cease."

INDEX.

LONDON: R. K. BURT AND CO., WINE OFFICE COURT, FLEET STREET.

FRIENDLESS AND FALLEN.

London Female Preventive & Reformatory Institution.

PRESIDENT—SIR WILLIAM ROSE, K.C.B.

Dear Reader,

I am assured of your deep heartfelt sympathy with suffering humanity in general, and in calling your attention to the subjoined advertisement, I doubt not but that you pity, and will help according to your means the efforts that are being put forth to protect and shelter, virtuous young women, when exposed to the perils and snares of temptation, and also to give a ray of hope to those who have erred from the paths of moral rectitude. It has been my privilege to labour for these classes for a quarter of a century, during which time I have daily heard tales of the bitterest sorrow, and seen manifestations of heartfelt repentance for sin. And still applicants for help press upon me and appeal by tears, dejected looks, as well as earnest language for help. Experience has taught me that in order to prosecute this mission of mercy with vigour help must be rendered from all classes of the community—the widow's mite, the working man's offering, the tradesman's donation, as well as the larger gift from those on whom the sun of prosperity has shone more bountifully, and Reader, I ask YOUR Contribution.

Very truly yours,

EDWARD W. THOMAS, *Secretary.*

OFFICE, 200, EUSTON ROAD, N.W.

The above Institution sustains Seven Homes,

200, EUSTON ROAD, N.W.; MILTON HOUSE, MAUDE GROVE, S.W.;

35, EDEN GROVE, HOLLOWAY ROAD, N.;

5, PARSON'S GREEN, FULHAM, S.W.; 195, HAMPSTEAD ROAD, N.W.;

AND

FOR FRIENDLESS YOUNG WOMEN OF GOOD CHARACTER,

7, PARSON'S GREEN, FULHAM, S.W.;

NIGHT REFUGE—37, Manchester Street, King's Cross, W.C.

10,790 poor young Women have been admitted to the above.

The whole Work is dependent upon Voluntary Support.

FUNDS ARE GREATLY NEEDED.

Donations may be sent in Postage Stamps.

EDWARD W. THOMAS, *Secretary.*

200, EUSTON ROAD, N.W.

Bankers : Messrs. BOSANQUET, SALT, & CO., 73, Lombard Street, E.C.

THE COLONIAL AND CONTINENTAL CHURCH SOCIETY.

THE PRINCIPLES OF THE SOCIETY are those of the Protestant and Reformed Church of England, and great pains are taken to send forth such Agents as know and love the truths of the Gospel.

COLONIAL.

THE OBJECTS OF THE SOCIETY are to send forth Clergymen, Catechists, and School Teachers to all parts of the world, wherever British residents are to be found.

The Society also sends Chaplains to minister to the wants of British sailors in foreign ports, the French settlers, the aboriginal Indians, and the coloured population in Canada.

The Agents Employed are:—Clergymen, 131; Catechists and Schoolmasters, 69; Female Teachers, 72; Total, 272.

The Society has Agents in the following 27 Colonial Dioceses:—

AMERICA.	Saskatchewan.	INDIA.	Grahamstown.
Newfoundland.		Calcutta. Madras.	Sierra Leone.
Nova Scotia.	WEST INDIES.		AUSTRALIA.
Fredericton.	Jamaica.	CHINA.	Goulburn. Bathurst.
Montreal. Quebec.	Nassau.	Victoria.	Perth. Tasmania.
Toronto. Huron.			Sydney. Melbourne.
Ontario. Algoma.	INDIAN OCEAN.	AFRICA.	
Rupert's Land.	Mauritius.	Capetown.	Gibraltar.

The Income for the year ending March 31, 1876, including funds raised and expended abroad, was £33,487 10s. 1d.

CONTINENTAL.

To send Chaplains to minister to residents and travellers on the Continent of Europe.

(1.) To settlements of artisans, miners, and others, scattered over the Continent.

(2.) To places where invalids resort in the winter months.

(3.) To English travellers in France, Germany, Italy, and Switzerland during the summer months.

The following Permanent Chaplaincies are connected with the Society:—

BELGIUM.	Chantilly.	GERMANY.	Milan.
Antwerp. Brussels.	Dieppe.	Barmen-Elberfeld.	Nervi (winter).
	Dunkerque.	Dusseldorf.	Pallanza.
FRANCE.	Honfleur.	Dresden.	San Remo (winter).
Amiens.	Hyères (winter).	Homburg.	Turin.
Arcachon.	Lille and Armentieres.	Memel.	
Ajaccio.	Lyons.	Munich.	SWITZERLAND.
Biarritz.	Paris.		Clarens (winter).
Bagneres de Bigorre.	Roubaix and Croix.	HOLLAND.	Villeneuve (winter)
Bordeaux.	Rouen and Sotteville.	The Hague.	SPAIN.
Boulogne.	St. Jean de Luz.	ITALY.	
Calais.	St. Servan.	Castellamare (winter).	Seville.
„ (St. Pierre.)	Tours.	Capri (winter)	IONIAN ISLANDS.
Cannes (winter).	Versailles.	Messina.	Zante.

The Society arranges for the regular performance of Divine Service during the summer season at the following places:—

FRANCE.	Innsbruck.	SWITZERLAND.	Heiden.
Aix les Bains.	Kissingen.	Aigle.	Interlaken.
Amphion.	Kreuznach.	Basle.	Le Prese (Poschiavo).
Chamonix.	Nuremberg	Bex.	Les Avants.
Eaux Bonnes.	Pyrmont.	Beatenberg.	Locarno.
Eaux Chaudes.	Schwalbach.	Brunnen.	Lucerne.
Fontainebleau.	Salzburg.	Champery Valais.	Maderanerthal.
Fecamp and Etretat.	St. Goar.	Chateaux d'Oex.	Neufchatel.
Luchon.	Strasburg.	Chaumont.	Ragatz.
Monnetier.	ITALY.	Chexbres.	Rhone Glacier.
St. Valery.	Bellagio.	Coire. [monts.	Riffelberg.
Trouville.	Bormio.	Comballaz aux Or-	Rigi-Kaltbad.
Vichy.	Courmayeur.	Davos am Platz.	Rossinieres.
	Stresa.	Diablerets.	Samaden.
GERMANY.	Varese.	Eggischorn.	Sepey.
Badenweiler.	Villa d'Este.	Felsenegg.	Stachelberg.
Berchtegaden.		Generoso.	Thun. Thusis.
Carlsbad.	NORWAY.	Giessbach.	Villars.
Constance.	Bergen.	Glion.	Zermatt.
Cortina.	Trondhjem.	Grindelwald.	Zweisimmen.

Contributions will be thankfully received at the OFFICES, 9. SERJEANTS' INN, FLEET STREET, LONDON, E.C., and at the Bank of Messrs. BARCLAY, BEVAN, & Co., 54, Lombard Street. Post Office Orders are payable to Rev. FRANCIS J. C. MORAN, B.D., Secretary.

WORKS BY DR. TALMAGE.

Crumbs Swept Up. Short Essays. Sixth and Cheaper Edition. Crown 8vo, cloth. 2s. 6d.

"Full of pointed, sagacious, and racy things."—*British Quarterly Review.*

"Points." Suggestive Passages, Incidents, and Illustrations from the Writings of T. DE WITT TALMAGE, D.D., of Brooklyn. With fine Portrait. Sixth Edition. Crown 8vo. 3s. 6d. cloth.

"The compiler has made a judicious selection, which will fully commend itself to English readers, of some of the brilliant passages and epigrammatically-expressed thoughts which are so marked a characteristic of Dr. Talmage's discourses. These are arranged under distinctive headings, and are preceded by a biographical sketch and an excellent steel engraving."—*Literary World.*

WORKS BY DR. CUYLER, of Brooklyn.

Heart Life. Sixth Thousand. 18mo, cloth. 1s. 6d.

"A little volume of fervid and spiritual addresses, often ingenious in conception, and always genial and gracious."—*British Quarterly Review.*

Thoughts for Heart and Life. Being a New Edition in One Volume of "Heart Life," "Heart Thoughts," and "Heart Culture." Fcap. 8vo, cloth. 3s. 6d.

Mr. Spurgeon says:—"Good things, strikingly put, abound in his pleasant pages."

The Highway of Salvation. By H. K. WOOD ("A Glasgow Merchant"), author of "Heavenly Love and Earthly Echoes." Third Thousand. 1s. 6d. cloth.

"It teaches very simply and lovingly the truth as it is in Jesus. The writer has carefully selected some very interesting anecdotes in illustration of his different chapters."—*Daily Review.*

Children Reclaimed for Life: the Story of Dr. Barnardo's Work in London. By the Author of "Romance of the Streets," "Byeways of Two Cities," &c. With Illustrations. Fourth Thousand. 3s. 6d. cloth elegant.

Talking to the Children. By ALEXANDER MACLEOD. Sixth Edition. 3s. 6d. cloth.

"An exquisite work. Divine truths are here presented in simple language, illustrated by parable and anecdote at once apt and beautiful."—*Evangelical Magazine.*

Nothing but Leaves. A Story. By SARAH DOUDNEY. Second Edition. 5s. cloth elegant.

"One of the most charming and exquisitely-told tales that we ever had the pleasure of perusing."—*Literary World.*

The Perils of Orphanhood; or, Frederica and her Guardians. By the Author of "Christie Redfern's Troubles," &c. Second Edition. 5s. cloth elegant.

"An exceedingly well-told story, full of incidents of an attractive character."—*Public Opinion.*

LONDON: HODDER & STOUGHTON, 27, PATERNOSTER ROW.

ELECTRICITY IS LIFE

PULVERMACHER'S IMPROVED
GALVANIC CHAIN-BANDS, &c.

Approved by the Academy of Medicine of Paris and other Medical
Faculties Abroad. Have stood the Test of ...

Check Out More Titles From HardPress Classics Series In this collection we are offering thousands of classic and hard to find books. This series spans a vast array of subjects – so you are bound to find something of interest to enjoy reading and learning about.

Subjects:
Architecture
Art
Biography & Autobiography
Body, Mind &Spirit
Children & Young Adult
Dramas
Education
Fiction
History
Language Arts & Disciplines
Law
Literary Collections
Music
Poetry
Psychology
Science
…and many more.

Visit us at www.hardpress.net